MEET DOROTHY DAY

Meet Dorothy Day

Champion of the Poor

Woodeene Koenig-Bricker

CHARIS

SERVANT PUBLICATIONS
ANN ARBOR, MICHIGAN

Charis books is an imprint of Servant Publications especially designed to serve Roman Catholics.

Servant Publications Mission Statement

We are dedicated to publishing books that spread the gospel of Jesus Christ, help Christians to live in accordance with that gospel, promote renewal in the church, and bear witness to Christian unity.

Published by Servant Publications
PO Box 8617
Ann Arbor, Michigan 48107
www.servantpub.com

Cover design: Paul Higdon, Minneapolis, Minn.

02 03 04 05 10 9 8 7 6 5 4 3 2 1

Printed in the United States of America
ISBN 1-56955-332-7

Library of Congress Cataloging-in-Publication Data

Koenig-Bricker, Woodeene.
  Meet Dorothy Day : champion of the poor / Woodeene Koenig-Bricker.
      p. cm.
Includes bibliographical references.
  ISBN 1-56955-332-7 (alk. paper)
  1. Day, Dorothy, 1897-1980. 2. Catholics--United States--Biography.
3. Catholic Worker Movement--History--20th century. I. Title.
  BX4705.D283 K64 2002
  267'.182'092--dc21

2002009344

Contents

Introduction

I knew very little about Dorothy Day when I began this book. I was dimly aware that she had been a communist, procured an abortion, and borne a daughter outside of marriage before her almost Augustinian conversion to Catholicism. I also knew she had protested the Vietnam War and had spent her life taking care of the poor—all of which had made her a prominent, albeit controversial, figure in the Church.

Her life just didn't make much impact in the mountains of Montana where I grew up. The inspiring biographies we heard from Sr. Mary St. Chester and the others at St. Anthony Grade School focused more on traditional religious figures such as Fr. Pierre-Jean De Smet, who evangelized the Blackfoot, and the brave missionaries who risked their lives in China. We rarely heard about steely-jawed socialists who worked in soup kitchens in the Bowery.

I knew even less about the newspaper Day published, *The Catholic Worker*. As a student I once had to go to the home of a family who was often praised for their work with the poor. I had heard they were involved in promoting *The Catholic Worker*, although I had no idea what *The Catholic Worker* was.

When I entered their home, I was appalled. Several runny-nosed children pawed at my skirt, the only furnishings in sight were several upended boxes, the whole place stank of dirty diapers, and a decrepit old lady lunged at me from a doorway, babbling incoherently. The couple didn't seem to notice the chaos, but I was shocked and appalled. (Not to mention a little scared!)

I decided that if that's what it meant to be a Catholic Worker, God spare me. I grabbed whatever package I had come there to pick up and literally ran out of the house. I had no interest in learning anything more about whatever this *Catholic Worker* was that they were promulgating.

When I grew up, I would occasionally hear something about Dorothy Day and the Catholic Worker movement on the news. But other than a few passing mentions, she was completely off my spiritual and secular radar. So, in a sense, I came to this project with what is called in Zen a "beginner's mind." I had no preconceived notions about Dorothy Day, and other than a fading memory of some Catholic Workers, whatever that meant, no expectations of what she would be like.

At first I was a bit daunted by the sheer volume of her writings, and even now I make no claims to have read all her own words and certainly not the plethora of books written about her. That would take nearly a lifetime in and of itself! It is certainly beyond the scope of this work to write a comprehensive biography and, besides, others with greater talent than I possess have done so admirably.

In any case, in order to introduce her to you, I needed to be introduced to her myself. So, I began to read ... and read ... and read. I started with her famous autobiography *The Long Loneliness* and ended with her reflections in *The Catholic Worker* newspaper. (I soon figured out what it was!) In between, I read some more.

As I struggled to understand this complex woman, I was at times put off by her radicalism, which almost felt like fanaticism. Instead of being inspired by the way she chose God before her common-law-husband, Forster, I felt myself sympathizing with him, a man who had "married" one girl and ended up with quite another. I winced at the thought of her getting all her clothes from secondhand bins (even though I've been known to cheer gleefully over bargains at resale stores). I cowered mentally at the thought of her being arrested yet another time. I even became judgmental about her long habit of smoking.

Partway through my reading and reflecting, I actually found myself disliking her. I told a friend she was the sort of person I might like to hear give a talk, but I wouldn't want her for my next-door neighbor. To be honest, I found her not just bracing, but a bit abrasive as well. That tight-set jaw and piercing stare were a little too much for me.

It wasn't until almost the end of my time with her, as I began to collect the quotes that comprise the final chapter of this little work, that I found myself softening. There is something almost mystical in typing another person's words. As your fingers race across the keyboard to form words that are not yours, you begin to understand the mind that originally created the thoughts.

It becomes a most intimate connection. Gradually, the more I typed, the more I understood what motivated this remarkable woman. And the more I understood, the more I appreciated her.

I warmed up to her even more as I struggled to decide what of her complex life and many friendships to include and what to omit. I discovered she had the same difficulty when she wrote. "How to understand people, portray people—that is the problem," she wrote in *Loaves and Fishes*. "Often one is accused of not telling the truth because one can tell only part of the truth ... how to write honestly, without failing in charity." How true, I found myself nodding in agreement!

I had just reached the point where I was begrudgingly admiring her and her work when I experienced what can only be evidence of God's sense of humor. I had gone onto the Internet to check a quote and noticed a link to the latest Catholic Worker House to be established in the United States. Clicking on it, I was stunned to see faces of my fellow parishioners! I knew that my parish had been working to establish a safe residence for young street kids, but until that moment I didn't realize that the John Bosco House we were funding was a Catholic Worker "House of Hospitality." I can only imagine that Dorothy was having a good chuckle over my astonishment.

However, I can't say that I truly *liked* Dorothy Day until near the end of the project, when I found something she wrote about working as a journalist. I, too, was trained as a journalist and have spent my entire life wandering with words. As I read her lines, something transformative happened. I almost felt her presence, in that strange and miraculous union we call the communion of saints. Her words became mine, although she says it better than I ever could:

If I have failed to give credit where credit is due, if I have neglected some aspects of the work in stressing others, I beg pardon of my readers, I am a journalist not a biographer, not a *book* writer....

This book is the work of a journalist who writes because it is her talent; it has been her means of livelihood and it is sent out with the hopes that it will sell, so that the bills will be paid.... "Life," said St. Teresa, "is but a night spent in an uncomfortable inn, crowded together with other wayfarers." There are bills to pay at an inn, of course, and they are one of the reasons which led me to send this manuscript forth, in the care of St. Joseph, patron of all families. May God bless it, and you who read it.

What can I add to that except to say: *Amen.*

ONE

IN THE BEGINNING

The lanky fourteen-year-old girl with oddly slanting almond eyes huddled over her books, her straight brown hair draping bony shoulders. "*Femina, feminae, feminam ...*" She forced the Latin declensions into her memory as the hissing coal fire in the kitchen grate tried futilely to battle the biting Chicago winter.

Changed and fed, her eight-month-old brother cooed happily beside her. The rest of the family—her other two brothers, sister, and parents—were still asleep; small wonder, for it was barely past 4:30 A.M. The young girl had been up since four, when her mother had unceremoniously dumped little John in her room, returning to her husband and their undisturbed slumber.

Forgoing her own need for rest, his sister had played with the baby until he grew hungry, then slipped into the icy kitchen to build a fire, heat a bottle, and tend to her by-now-fussy charge. For the next hour and a half, she would study—mostly Latin and Greek—until waking her siblings, fixing them breakfast, and heading off to school. While her parents were well rested, she was lucky to get four solid hours of sleep a night.

Later she would write in one of her autobiographies:

Every morning the next two school years, long before dawn, my mother used to bring him in to my bed. Since my father did not

11

get to bed until two in the morning, it was very important that the baby be kept quiet so that his sleep should be undisturbed. The child was difficult to put to bed and every night I rocked him to sleep, singing hymns to him from my Episcopal hymn-book.... But the very hardship of taking care of him, the hours I put in with him, made me love him the more.[1]

Even then, the link between sacrifice and love motivated her, as it would for the rest of her life. Eulogized many years later by *The New York Times* as a "nonviolent social radical of luminous personality," and by Daniel Berrigan, S.J., as "American to the marrow," she was a romantic, a rebel, and above all a Roman Catholic.

She was Dorothy Day.

* * *

If you like your saints sanitized, Dorothy Day isn't for you. Never in the history of the American Catholic Church has there been a woman quite like the angular-jawed, chain-smoking, outspoken journalist and cofounder of the Catholic Worker movement. A suffragette, anarchist, and communist in her youth, she ran through a series of lovers and two marriages (one common-law), had an abortion, and raised her only daughter as a single parent—just for starters. She championed the rights of workers to strike, even when they were striking against the Archdiocese of New York; was jailed at least eleven times for civil disobedience; counseled draft resistance; refused to pay taxes; protested the Vietnam War; and never voted.

She also had a passionate love for the Divine Office and the Eucharist, made regular retreats, and counted as close personal friends such luminaries of the faith as the Trappist monk Thomas Merton.

She once marched in favor of birth control, and she once wrote: "Let us be honest and confess that it is the social order which we wish to change. The workers are never going to be satisfied, no matter how much pay they get, no matter what their hours are."[2] Yet the same woman also later wrote: "Prayer is the answer, it is the clasp of the hand, the joy and keen delight in the consciousness of that Other. Indeed it is like falling in love."[3]

For many saints who underwent profound change—including St. Francis of Assisi, for whom Dorothy had a particular love and devotion—their pre-conversion life can be summed up in a few sentences to something of this effect: They were sinners and mended their ways. The specifics of their former lives are not essential; it is their after-faith life that matters.

Not so with Dorothy. In her autobiography, she says: "My life has been divided into two parts,"[4] and indeed it was. In order to understand the elderly woman who marched with Cesar Chavez on behalf of migrant workers, it is essential to meet the bobbed-haired young visionary who tossed back glass after glass of whiskey with Eugene O'Neill and plotted the overthrow of Western civilization with other idealistic revolutionaries in dimly lit, smoke-filled saloons.

Family of Origin

Dorothy's family of origin was what modern psychotherapists would undoubtedly label "dysfunctional," although it was probably fairly typical in its time. Her father, John Day, was a Scotch-Irish journalist specializing in horseracing. He was a heavy drinker, bound heart and mind to bloodlines and betting sheets, who demanded his wife's full and exclusive attention and alternated between ignoring his children and drawing implacable lines in the sand over which he dared them to cross.

Her mother, Grace Satterlee Day, was characterized by Dorothy as "strong and cheerful" with a "temperament which helped her through much hardship and uncertainty." A less-charitable sort might have said she was in denial. No matter how desperate the family situation (and it was mighty desperate at times), she would always end her day by bathing and dressing in a fluttering silk negligee with embroidered flowers and storks to retire to the intimacy of the boudoir with her husband. The demands of her spouse—he forbade the children to have guests because it bothered his privacy; he insisted that Dorothy tend to her brother because the baby's crying disturbed his sleep, and besides, he didn't want his wife to be away from him in the night— came before all else.

Nevertheless, Dorothy remembered her mother with kindness, focusing on her gentle spirit and genuine desire to help her children see the good in all situations. She forewent criticism of her father as well, apparently adhering to the principle, "If you can't say something nice, don't say anything at all." The closest Dorothy came to criticizing her family was to say years later, "Our parents did nothing to offer us distractions and entertainment. We were forced to meet our moods and overcome them."[5]

Dorothy was the third of the couple's five children. Donald was born in 1895, followed by Sam Houston in 1896, and Dorothy on November 8, 1897, in Brooklyn. Two years later sister Della arrived, and nearly twelve years afterward, little John.

On the Path to God

Nothing in Dorothy's early life would have served as an indicator of her trajectory toward God. Her father, raised a Congregationalist, was a self-avowed atheist, and her erstwhile Episcopalian mother followed his lead in religion, as in everything else. The subject of religion simply was nonexistent in the Day household.

Of her early training, Dorothy wrote: "We prayed at school every morning, bowing our heads on our desks and saying the Our Father, and I can still smell the varnish, and see the round circle of moisture left by my mouth on the varnish as I bent close to the desk. In trying to remember my religious experiences, that is all I can recall of formal prayer during those years."[6]

In 1904, John Day moved his family to California, where he had a job writing racetrack news. It was there, in Berkeley, that Dorothy had her first real exposure to any kind of faith. An inquisitive child who read from the age of four, she discovered a Bible in the attic of their rented house, and she spent one long Saturday reading it. She later recalled "the sense of holiness in holding the book" in her hands. "I did not know then," she said, "that the Word in the Book and the Word in the flesh of Christ's humanity were the same, but I felt I was handling something holy."[7]

A few years later, when she was eight, they were living next door to the Reeds, a Methodist family. Dorothy became, in her own words, "disgustingly, proudly pious." She sang hymns with vigor, knelt by her bed to pray, and quizzed her mother as to why their family was not more devout.

Her religious fervor was short-lived when Naomi Reed, who was Dorothy's age, was forbidden to play with her when it came out that

Dorothy had called her brother a bad name and thrown something at him during an argument. Dorothy was unperturbed. She took up with "a tough gang of kids who stayed out after dark and didn't mind their mothers" and "had a very good time indeed." So much for religion, in her mind.

Her inchoate fervor was further trampled by the great San Francisco earthquake of 1909. Although her family escaped direct harm, Dorothy had her first taste of helping the needy as she watched her mother care for the homeless and hungry, and she soon experienced grinding poverty firsthand. The company John Day worked for went broke in the aftermath of the disaster, so he packed up his family and moved to Chicago.

There, they lived in a miserable flat over a bar and ate nothing but potato soup, bread, bananas, tea, and jelly. Her father failed to find work and so began to write a novel, taking over the living room and littering it with paper, cigarette butts, and glasses of whiskey. The novel never sold, and John Day dashed off little pieces about horseracing to keep his family from being tossed on the streets.

Impulse Toward Catholicism

It was in the midst of this squalor that Dorothy had her "first impulse toward Catholicism." Observing the mother of one of her playmates kneeling in daily prayer, she was swept in "a warm burst of love," recognizing that the joy in this woman's life came from her relationship with God. Dorothy gained a bit more knowledge about Catholics from an Irish family who lived nearby.

The oldest daughter in that family, Lenore Clancey,[8] introduced

Dorothy to the lives of the saints, which immediately inspired the impressionable young girl. "I ... remember my feeling of lofty enthusiasm, and how my heart almost burst with desire to take part in such high endeavor," she wrote.[9] She was so taken with the idea of sainthood that she insisted that she and her younger sister Della "practice being saints." Della, it must be noted, was far less enthusiastic than Dorothy about being half-frozen with the cold and kneeling in prayer until her knees ached.

About this time, Dorothy began her lifelong love affair with the Psalms, a passion that would abide even during her anarchist Bohemian years. An Episcopal priest learned that Mrs. Day had been raised in that faith and pressed the Days to allow their children to attend his church. Her brothers sang in the choir (she greatly admired their cassocks and surplices and was attracted to a blond boy soloist), and Dorothy began to memorize psalms, saying, "I had never heard anything so beautiful as the *Benedicite* and the *Te Deum*. The words have remained with me ever since."[10]

A few years before her death, she would reiterate that sentiment:

It is then that I turn most truly for solace, for strength to endure, to the Psalms. I may read them without understanding, and mechanically at first, but I do believe they are the Word, and Scripture, on the one hand, and the Eucharist, the Word made Flesh, on the other, have in them that strength which no power on earth can withstand.[11]

Somewhere along the way, Dorothy was baptized and confirmed, but neither event made much impression on her. Being an Episcopalian never really "took." When she suffered from migraines, her mother explored Christian Science on her behalf, and Dorothy found the teachings of Mary Baker Eddy nearly as interesting as the preaching of the Episcopal rector of the Church of Our Savior—which is to say, not very interesting at all.

The World Outside

Far more interesting to her was her crush on a musician who lived down the street, which stirred her first sexual desires; and the birth of her youngest brother, John, which kindled her deep maternal instinct, and whose rearing she pretty much took over. The winds of the family's fortune blew warmer when John Sr. got a job as a sports editor. They moved to a better neighborhood.

Dorothy loved to push her little brother in his carriage, and even the responsibility of his nighttime care was a source of joy. She spent her high school years studying, watching over John Jr., and reading ravenously—Darwin, Kant, Spinoza, Jack London, Upton Sinclair, Sinclair Lewis, and Dostoevsky among the many. Upton Sinclair's *The Jungle* pricked her conscience, and she walked on Chicago's South Side, exposing herself to the reality of America's urban poverty.

To outward appearances she continued to be devoutly Christian. In a letter to a friend, she wrote:

> The tears come to my eyes, when I think how often I have gone through the bitter struggles and then succumbed to sin just as peace was in sight. And how after I fell how far away it fled. Poor weak creatures that we are, yet God is our Father and God is love, ever present to enfold us and comfort us and hold us up....

I know it is foolish to try to be so Christlike—but God says we can—why else His command, "Be ye therefore perfect?"[12]

She had the words down pat, but lest anyone think she was ready for canonization at age fifteen, she pointed out that she wrote that way only to impress the friend who was deeply religious and sentimental.

A Break With Religion

Thus it comes as no great surprise that almost as abruptly as her interest in organized religion waxed, it waned. One day, while making fudge with her sister (surreptitiously so that their father wouldn't find out and have his peace disturbed), she told Della she was "sick and tired of religion" and suggested they sneak off to the movies. Della, who had never been all that enthused about piety, readily agreed.

Dorothy later recalled: "My belief in God remained firm and I continued to read the New Testament regularly but I felt it was no longer necessary to go to church." She would not feel the need again for some time.

However, the "Hound of Heaven," as the poet Francis Thompson has called him, was on her trail. She would later write: "'All my life I have been haunted by God,' a character in one of Dostoevsky's books says. And that is the way it was with me."[13]

TWO

GROWING UP RADICAL

Some people look back on their high school days with fondness, recalling graduation as one of the high points of their lives. For Dorothy, her graduation from Walker High School in June 1914 was of so little import that she never mentioned it in any of her voluminous writings. What did excite her was the three hundred dollar college scholarship that she had won from the *Chicago Examiner*. (Ironically, her father worked on the rival newspaper, and later in her life, Dorothy would urge boycotting of Hearst publications.) And so, in early September, the lanky sixteen-year-old left her family to attend the University of Illinois at Urbana.

College Days

In college, Dorothy was an indifferent student, finding most classes boring and suffering great pangs of homesickness, especially for her baby brother. Ordinary student life held little appeal, for already her heart was being drawn toward the radical fringes.

She took up smoking—which she didn't give up until her late forties—and began to swear. She admitted that this shocked her as much as it did her churchgoing friends, but she felt it was an important gesture she had to make in order to distance herself from organized religion.

"My faith had nothing in common with that of Christians around me," she wrote.[1]

Indeed, her decision to leave behind any religious sentiment was done, as they say, with "malice aforethought."

A professor whom I much admired made a statement in class—I shall always remember it—that religion was something which had brought great comfort to people throughout the ages, so that we ought not to criticize it. I do not remember his exact words, but from the way he spoke of religion the class could infer that the strong did not need such props. In my youthful arrogance, in my feeling that I was one of the strong, I felt then for the first time that religion was something that I must ruthlessly cut out of my life.

Ironically, in light of her later life, she added, "I felt at the time that religion would only impede my work."[2]

In the first occurrence of a repeating pattern of moving from job to job, Dorothy found work here and there to supplement her meager scholarship. She lived with families, doing the laundry and tending the children, in exchange for room and board. She began to dabble in writing columns for the local paper—columns that often offered criticism of the social order.

An awareness of the suffering of others—the sick, the infirm, the disabled, the unemployed, the unemployable, and the destitute—was beginning to awaken. Her lifelong passion for the poor was sprouting. "I was in love with masses," she later wrote. "I do not remember that I was articulate or reasoned about this love, but it warmed and filled my heart."[3]

The Radical Emerges

The familiar social activities of student life—football games, sororities and their ilk—were of no interest to this serious young girl. She was attracted by the concept of political reform and joined the "Socialist Study Club," a women's branch of the University Socialists Club. But she found the discussions excruciatingly dull and seldom could bring herself to attend the meetings. The process of formal education did little for her, either, and she skipped classes at will. Despite her lackluster efforts, she passed all her courses save one—biology.

The bright light in her two years at college was her close friendship with Rayna Simons, a resplendent, red-haired Jewish girl who introduced her to a circle of literary friends and gave her some much needed financial assistance. Dorothy remembered the time she and Rayna spent together in college as "an idyllic year," and she credited much of it to Rayna. "I must have known that such friendships come only rarely in a lifetime and I treasured every hour we had together."[4]

The direction her life might have taken if she had continued in college can only be speculated about. Instead, when her father took a new job in New York, Dorothy, who had thought herself ready for independence, said she could not bear being so far from her family, so she followed them to the Big Apple.

How much of her decision was rooted in homesickness and how much was based in dislike of school is debatable. What is certain is that her days of formal education had ended. With absolutely no desire to finish college, she was determined to launch her career as a journalist.

It was not a happy moment for her father, even though he was a newspaper man himself. It was bad enough to have a chain-smoking, swearing, socialist daughter—but one who insisted at working in what he considered a masculine endeavor? It was all too much, and John Day "made it plain no daughter of his was going to work and live at home."

A Journalist From the Beginning

When Dorothy landed a job with the *Call*, the city's only socialist daily newspaper, she was truly on her own.

At age eighteen all of life is an adventure, and so it was for Dorothy. She agreed to work for the first month for five dollars a week so she could write about what it was like to live on such scanty income. Then, if she impressed her boss, she would be hired on permanently for forty-eight dollars a month.

If she had thought she had experienced want during her family's hard times, it was nothing compared to what she encountered in New York's East Side. Her less-than-sufficient wages meant she was plunged headlong into destitution. Her first apartment, just a tiny room, was heated only with a one-burner gas stove. The feather bed was filled with vermin, the wind moaned down the airshaft, the stench outside her door woke her at night, and cats shrieked the howls of the damned in the hallway.

She didn't stay there long, however. Soon she rented a room in the parish hall of an old Episcopal church. This move was the beginning of another pattern. Dorothy would spend all her days "on pilgrimage," as she would later dub her column in the newspaper she founded, never having a permanent home and always moving on as her spirit— and the Spirit—prompted.

Dorothy did impress the editor, and she was hired as a general reporter. The *Call* was never quite sure what it was calling about, although it espoused general socialist tendencies. Dorothy threw herself into the various causes she investigated and reported on them all with the enthusiasm of the young and idealistic. She took in great, gasping gulps of "socialism, syndicalism [the International Workers of the World, called the I.W.W. or Wobblies] and anarchism" and breathed out social reform and revolution.

She wasn't entirely sure what she espoused; all she knew was that she was for radical change. "I wavered between my allegiance to socialism, syndicalism, and anarchism. When I read Tolstoi, I was an anarchist. Ferrer with his schools, Kropotkin with his farming communes, the I.W.W.'s with their solidarity, their unions, these all appealed to me."[5]

She also initially championed birth control, embracing the idea as the solution to the world's problems of poverty and the oppression of women. About this same time, she gave her overt approval as well to premarital sex, shocking her mother, with whom she remained in contact. (It is likely Dorothy was still a virgin at the time. She remained appalled by the notion of promiscuity throughout her entire life.)

Through her work, she came in daily touch with the misery of the poor, and her heart began its lifelong ache to make a real difference in their lives. Yet, in later years, she questioned her true motives:

> I do not really know myself as I was then. I do not know how sincere I was in my love of the poor and my desire to serve them. I know that I was in favor of the works of mercy as we know them, regarding the drives for food and clothing for strikers in the light of justice, and an aid in furthering the revolution. But I was bent on following the journalist's side of the work. I wanted

the privileges of the woman and the work of the man, without following the work of the woman. I wanted to go on picket lines, to go to jail, to write, to influence others and so make my mark on the world. How much ambition and how much self-seeking there was in all this![6]

However, then as always, Dorothy was curiously apolitical—if someone devoted to the overthrow of social order can be said to be apolitical. Years later she tried to explain her detachment:

Life on a newspaper, whether radical or conservative, makes one lose all sense of perspective at the time. You are carried along in a world of events, writing, reporting, with no time at all for thought or reflection.... Nothing stood out in my mind. We reporters worked from twelve noon until twelve at night, covering meetings and strikes. We walked on picket lines; we investigated starvation and death in the slums. Our function as journalists seemed to be to build up a tremendous indictment against the present system, a daily tale of horror which would have a cumulative effect of forcing the workers to rise in revolution.[7]

With her fellow socialists, she celebrated the first days of the Russian revolution as the harbinger of a new way of life and justice.

I joined with those thousands in reliving the first days of the revolt in Russia. I felt the exultation, the joyous sense of victory of the masses as they sang "Ei Euchnjem," the workers' hymn of Russia. It seemed to signify that "like the flowing of the river, is the progress of human events," as the *Call* said next day in a story which went on to describe the song as a "mystic gripping melody of struggle, a cry for world peace and human brotherhood."[8]

A Social Rebel in a Bohemian World

Revolution energized her, but the rest of the world politic was relatively unimportant to her. Ideas, not events, were her venue. While America was being swept up in the political furor surrounding President Wilson's declaration of war in 1917, she dismissed it as anticlimactic. She was much more interested in a dance called the "Anarchist Ball" to be held in Greenwich Village.

On such a seemingly insignificant axis spin the wheels of life. At this dance, an acquaintance of disrepute made an advance she deemed inappropriate; she slapped him; her date—a fellow reporter from the *Call*—criticized her; and, as a result, she never returned to her job. Instead she went to work for *The Masses*, a socialist magazine that featured the writing of such literati as Upton Sinclair and Vachel Lindsay.

The slap she gave at the dance she would later consider a slap in her own face. She never forgot it and remembered it with shame.

I was neither a Christian nor a pacifist, and I certainly acted like neither. I recall this tiny incident because it illustrates a point that has since come up many times in our work with others. Our desire for justice for ourselves and for others often complicates the issue, builds up factions and quarrels. Worldly justice and unworldly justice are quite different things.[9]

At this time in her life, though, Dorothy was intent on seeking worldly justice, for she earnestly believed that it was within humanity's power to save the world. If only the poor would realize their power, they would usher in the necessary changes to make this a heaven on earth. It was her job to help ignite their imaginations and set the revolution in motion.

And what of the Hound of Heaven? He continued to sniff at Dorothy's trail, but far enough in the distance so that she could only catch faint echoes of his bay in the works of Tolstoi and Dostoevsky.

THREE

THE GREATEST SORROW OF ALL

It is the year 1917. Woodrow Wilson is president. Jeannette Rankin of Montana has just become the first woman to serve in the House of Representatives. The United States is on the brink of declaring war on Germany, thus catapulting the nation into World War I. The Bolsheviks led by Lenin have seized power in Russia.

Now imagine that you have just turned twenty-one. You and your circle of friends savor being at the center of Bohemian life in Greenwich Village. You spend long evenings drinking and talking about establishing a new world order. You believe that "all the world's your oyster," and soon—not quite soon enough to suit you, but soon—revolution will sweep the globe, and you will be in the vanguard of the change.

That's exactly where Dorothy found herself after having abandoned the *Call.*

Calling *The Masses*

For a few weeks after that fateful dance, she worked for the Anti-Conscription League, until she secured a position with *The Masses,* a monthly left-wing magazine that opposed American involvement in the European war. It was here that she sharpened her blue editing pencil, since the regular editor, Floyd Dell, was inclined to wander off to work on a novel he was writing, and the assistant editor was prone to long spells of dreamy introspection. Young and inexperienced as she was, Dorothy became, in effect and often in reality, the editor of the publication.

She might have happily stayed there for a long time since *The Masses* suited both her idealism and her political stance, but the United States Post Office had other plans in mind: The magazine's mailing permit was rescinded. The government confiscated back issues, unpublished manuscripts, and subscriber lists and charged the editors with sedition under the 1917 Espionage Act. Dorothy was not accused of any crime because her name did not appear on any of the printed articles, but with the demise of *The Masses,* she once again found herself afloat on life's current.

But not for long. An old friend arrived like a bit of flotsam on the high tide to convince her to join in a suffragist picket march on the White House. Dorothy, who never voted and was never terribly interested in politics except where it intersected with social justice, was anxious to make a stand against the government as a protest to the wartime draft that had recently been enacted. So she agreed. The march was short-lived, and Dorothy soon found herself in jail for the first time in her life, although it would hardly be the last time she would be imprisoned for her anti-war pacifism.

In Prison for the First Time

Imprisonment was not the glamorous stand against capitalistic imperialism and warmongering that she had imagined. It was a miserable, boring experience made the worse by a hunger strike she felt compelled to join. She fell into depression, writing:

> I lost all consciousness of any cause. I had no sense of being a radical, making a protest against a government, carrying on a nonviolent revolution. I could feel only darkness and desolation all around me.... The futility of life came over me so that I could not weep but only lie there in blank misery.[1]

In the midst of her misery she asked for and was given a Bible. Immediately she turned to the Psalms she had loved as a child and clung to their comfort.

At the same time, her lofty idea that religion was only for the weak haunted her, and she vacillated between reaching out to God and pushing him away. When she and the others were finally released by presidential order, she was embarrassed by what she viewed as a descent into religious sentiment: "I had seen myself too weak to stand alone, too weak to face the darkness of that punishment cell without crying out, and I was ashamed and again rejected religion that had helped me when I had been brought to my knees by my suffering."[2]

The Hound of Heaven

Upon her return to New York, Dorothy cast off her recent religious predilection and plunged into Village life. One of her favorite haunts was the Provincetown Playhouse, where Eugene O'Neill had a play in rehearsal. After the rehearsals, she and a gang of regulars would retire to a saloon nicknamed the Hell Hole. "No one ever wanted to go to bed and no one ever wished to be alone," she later commented.[3]

It was there, in the smoky darkness, amid the clank of glasses and drunken laughter, that the Hound crept closer. It was also there that she first, literally, heard the "Hound of Heaven." Eugene O'Neill knew all of Francis Thompson's poem by heart, and when sufficiently intoxicated, he "would sit there, black and dour, his head sunk as he intoned" the story of God's relentless pursuit of the soul. Dorothy was inexplicably fascinated by the idea, realizing that "sooner or later I would have to pause in the mad rush of living and remember my first beginning and last end."

But not quite yet. True, many mornings, as she came home from drinking all night or going to parties and dances, she would slip into the back pew of St. Joseph's Church and listen to early morning Mass. She had no intention of joining a church—and certainly not the Catholic Church—but the need to pray would sometimes overwhelm her, and she would hide in the still darkness, lifting her heart to Something or Someone she did not understand, yet could not escape.

A New Career

However much comfort she derived from these surreptitious morning visits, she also was young, idealistic, and determined not to succumb to religion—what Communists called the "opiate of the people." The pathos of the time drove her to do something more constructive about the war than merely lament the fighting while she had a glass of whiskey with friends. "Now that we are in the thick of war and there is so much work to be done, I might as well try to do some of it instead of sitting around playing at writing," she wrote to a friend. She applied to and was accepted into the nursing program at King's County Hospital in Brooklyn with her sister Della. She discovered she enjoyed nursing, not the least because she loved to nurture and was particularly pleased to serve the least fortunate.

Despite, or perhaps because of, her daily dealings with disease and death, she relished the beauty in the common, ordinary things of life and earth. That pleasure would become one of the characteristics of her life and her writing. A poet and naturalist by temperament, she wrote in her autobiographies not just about bedpans and enemas but also about the sparrows and starlings and the large brindle cat who slunk under the branches with her eye on a pigeon. She also admitted that although nice ladies didn't smoke at the time, she would steal a furtive (and much enjoyed) puff behind the powerhouse and laundry.

Still the Hound advanced. "There was another beauty which came into my life at that time," she wrote. She began to attend early morning Mass on Sundays with a fellow student, admitting: "I felt that it was necessary for man to worship, that he was most truly himself when engaged in that act." She found the service inspiring, but not inspiring enough to commit to joining an organized religion.

It was also the first and last season in her life that she would not write. Ever restless and not one to remain long at any job, she tried vainly to convince herself that nursing was her call in life, but even as she made beds and tended victims of the great flu epidemic, she grew increasingly discontent. "A longing to write, to be pursuing the career of journalist which I had chosen for myself, swept over me so that even though I loved the work in the hospital, I felt that it was a second choice and not my vocation," she wrote in one of her autobiographies. "My work was to write and there was no time for that where I was. I was rebelling too against the discipline, long hours and steady hard work."4

But before she left nursing to return full-time to the typewriter, she experienced what she would always consider her greatest sorrow. And even though she would loathe to mention it in her later years, she would also remember it as her most appalling sin.

Love and Death

She fell in love—almost literally at first sight—with an orderly in one of the hospital kitchen wards. A rough-hewn man with a broken nose, Lionel Moise had been hauled into the hospital in a coma after some sort of drunken interlude, and after a week he had awakened from his stupor. Once he had recovered, he worked temporarily at the hospital to pay off his bill.

A heavy-drinking newspaper man who impressed even the likes of Ernest Hemingway with his abilities on the rewrite desk, Moise stirred something in Dorothy that no other man ever had. Despite his rugged edges and rampant alcoholism, he was quite the ladies' man, and Dorothy was determined to make him her first lover. They moved in together and had, by her account, a passionate albeit rocky love affair.

In the following days, they would separate, come back together, then separate again. At one point, Dorothy was so despondent she may have even attempted suicide. In any event, her life with Moise was tempestuous and tormented even before she discovered she was pregnant. When she learned she was "*enceinte*," she reacted as has many a young girl before and since—flinging herself on her bed wailing and pounding her fists into the pillow.

It was, to say the least, a most unfortunate turn of events. Moise had made no bones about the fact he did not want to be a father, and while Dorothy was deeply attracted to children, she was madly in love with him and unwilling to give him up. Considering her options, she ruled out both going home and going to a home for unwed mothers.

Dorothy eventually decided that her only recourse was an abortion. However, she delayed both taking that step and telling Moise that she was pregnant for a couple of months, perhaps hoping that he might grow accustomed to their life together and accept the idea of creating a family. It was not to be. In early September 1917, Moise told Dorothy that he was leaving her, and she informed him of her condition.

True to his word that he wanted absolutely nothing to do with fatherhood, he demanded that she have an abortion, telling her that he would come and get her when it was over. She visited a female abortionist, underwent the painful and frightening procedure alone, and then waited. Moise never arrived.

When she got back to their home after hailing a taxi, he was gone. He had left her a note advising her to marry a rich man because he would probably want to borrow some money from her when he returned. He also said that he had cashed a check on a closed account, leaving her the money to take care of herself for the next few weeks or until she returned to the hospital. His parting advice was that she should forget about him.

Although she was reluctant to discuss this part of her life, years later, in her column in *The Catholic Worker*, she would write about abortion in general:

I am reminded when I hear these middle-aged liberals sounding off on sexual and other fleshy freedoms, of some of the men of the same middle-class, middle-aged liberal background who used to hang around Greenwich Village probing into and inciting the young people about them, to a free sex life as though hoping youth would not miss these ardors that they perhaps feel that they missed. Or perhaps they had not missed them but their pleasure in sex had been dimmed by just that sense of sin natural to man when he lets his lower nature take over irresponsibly. Some men have incited their own children to gratify their desires and to get rid of the fruit of their intercourse by abortion, as I know happened in two families. It is one thing not to judge others, and it is still another thing to expect men and women to live according to right reason, to seek wisdom and live by it. The wisdom of the flesh is treacherous indeed.[5]

For young Dorothy, her abortion was a personal tragedy. Near the end of her life, for seventy-six-year-old Dorothy, it had become a mysterious means of grace and transformative forgiveness.

And so, when it comes to divorce, birth control, abortion, I must write in this way. The teaching of Christ, the Word, must be upheld. Held up though one would think that it is completely beyond us—out of our reach, impossible to follow. I believe Christ is our Truth and is with us always. We may stretch towards it, falling short, failing seventy times seven, but forgiveness is always there. He is a kind and loving judge.... I believe in the Sacraments. I believe grace is conferred thru the Sacraments. I believe the priest is empowered to forgive sins. Grace is defined as "participation in the divine life," so little by little we are putting off the old man and putting on the new. Actually, "putting on Christ."[6]

The deliberate killing of her own child was the lowest point in Dorothy's entire life. She would never be the same again.

FOUR

LOVE IS THE MEASURE OF ALL

In both her autobiographies, *From Union Square to Rome* and *The Long Loneliness*, Dorothy glides over the next part of her life, explaining, "I find that there is little to say."[1] Yet it was not so much that there was little to say as it was that Dorothy did not want to talk about it—then or any time later.

A Radical Abroad

Little wonder; it was a miserable period. Despite Moise's shoddy treatment of her, she was still passionately in love with him. A few months after the end of the affair she married Barkeley Tobey, a man nearly twice her age, in what was patently a rebound—an attempt to forget. The newlyweds sailed to Europe, where they lived for the better part of a year in France and Italy, and Dorothy worked on her only published novel, a thinly disguised autobiography entitled *The Eleventh Virgin*.

Like so many other romantics before and since, she fell in love with the Isle of Capri, where she spent six months.

Forever after, the smell of Italian cooking, the sound of buzzing flies, the loud strong voices of my Italian neighbors, the taste of spaghetti and polenta and the sour red wine brought me back to the months I spent beside the Mediterranean or wandering around the streets of Naples, or driving on sightseeing trips behind the shabby horses with their voluble drivers.[2]

She was enamored with Italy, but her husband was quite another matter. Barkeley, like Moise, was a notorious ladies' man with an unsavory side. (When he died in 1964, he had been married eight times—with numerous other liaisons.) Although Dorothy never expounded on the details of their relationship, it was clear the marriage was doomed from the beginning. All she said was that she spent that year writing and "living through a time of [her] own personal joy and heartbreak and what happened in the world had little effect on [her]."[3]

Back in the States

Dorothy and Barkeley may have separated while still in Europe. In any case, it is certain that they promptly divorced upon their return to the States. Dorothy did not go back to New York. Instead she went to Chicago, where Moise was working for a newspaper, and tried to resume their affair.

She had never abandoned her dream that Moise would fall as deeply in love with her as she was with him, marry her, and give her a baby to replace the one she had aborted. He was apparently willing enough to take up with her, although not to live with her. She was undaunted, and with her attention once again riveted on the pursuit of Moise, she supported herself by drifting from job to job, working at Montgomery Ward's, in the public library, as a cashier in a restaurant, as an art model, and, as always, writing bits and snatches for publication.

The fact that he had other lovers did not seem to deter her from clutching at the straws of the relationship. In fact, one of his girlfriends forced Dorothy into what she would remember as "an unutterably horrifying experience." Mae Cramer, a former drug addict, attempted suicide when Moise jilted her, and in a moment of desperation she turned to Dorothy for help. When Dorothy spent the night with her in the rented room where she was recuperating, the two were arrested for prostitution.

Jailed Again

When she had been arrested in the suffragist march, Dorothy had been buoyed by her solidarity with the suffering poor of the world—"the glow at the beginning of working with others, at being part of a noble cause." This time in jail, however, things were different.

> [I] was a victim of my own imprudence, of my own carelessness of convention.... It was as ugly an experience as I ever wish to pass through, and a useful one. I do not think that ever again, no matter of what I am accused, can I suffer more than I did then of shame and regret, and self-contempt. Not only because I had been caught, found out, branded, publicly humiliated, but because of my own consciousness that I deserved it.[4]

She was, perhaps, a little harsh on herself since she was not—and never had been—a prostitute. Her only crimes were foolish imprudence and youthful thoughtlessness.

As it turns out, Mae Cramer had left the hospital where she was recovering from her overdose and ended up at a hotel run by the I.W.W. Women were not allowed there, and that night, in a "Red Raid" for suspected communists, the hotel was seized as a disorderly house. All the occupants, including Dorothy and Mae, were arrested.

The torment of being strip-searched and tossed into a cell with ladies of the evening was sheer anguish for Dorothy.

> I felt the sadness of sin, the unspeakable dreariness of sin from the first petty little self-indulgence to this colossal desire which howled through the metal walls! And yet I do not think I thought of these things as I thought of God while in the solitary confinement cell at Occoquan [after the suffragist march].[5] I just suffered desperately and desired to be freed from my sufferings, with a most urgent and selfish passion.[6]

A radical friend arranged for her release after two days and the case was dropped, but the horror of it haunted her for years. "I think that for a long time one is stunned by such experiences," she later wrote. "They seem to be quickly forgotten, but they leave a scar that is never removed."[7]

Catholic Influences Redux

The only bright spot in her bleak, Moise-centered universe was her friendship with two Catholic girls, Blanche and Bee, who introduced her to Catholic terminology and took her with them to novenas and missions. She later wrote:

I wondered why they never made any attempts to interest me in their faith. I felt that Catholicism was something rich and real and fascinating, but I felt outside, and though I went with them to the mission, it never occurred to them that I might want to talk to a priest. Of course they knew that my standards were not theirs, that I belonged to radical groups who had a different code of morals, who did not believe in God or if they did, felt no necessity for worship in an organized Church.[8]

Dorothy might have continued pining after Moise and drifting from job to job except that fate ... or the Hound ... intervened. Moise left for Wisconsin in the winter of 1923-24 under somewhat suspicious circumstances, taking with him the last shards of Dorothy's dreams. Finally, painfully, she allowed him to be wrenched from her heart.

Shortly afterwards, she and her sister Della moved to New Orleans, where Dorothy landed a job on a newspaper and reported on such notable events as "taxi dances." It was a time of relative happiness, as the two sisters enjoyed the New Orleans social scene and genial Southern poverty. Here, too, she obtained her first rosary, and when she wasn't busy, she would slip into the cathedral to pray the beads or to listen to Benediction. But regular churchgoing was still in her future.

One True Love

Dorothy's Southern interlude ended when her novel was published in April 1924, and she received twenty-five hundred dollars from the sale of the movie rights. Dorothy felt herself to be rich and moved back to

New York. There she purchased a little house on the west end of Staten Island and moved in with the second great love of her life, the man who finally made her forget Moise.

> The man I loved, with whom I entered into a common-law marriage, was an anarchist, an Englishman by descent, and a biologist.... [He] spent most of his time during World War I hospitalized with influenza, from which he did not recover until the war was over. When I met him he was out of uniform and had begun to get back some of the seventy-five pounds he had lost during his hospital year. His friends were mostly liberals and his sympathies were decentralist and anti-industrialist, though he loved the machine and the illusion of progress.[9]

His name was Forster Batterham. They fished together, walked on the beach for miles, and collected marine specimens. As she put it: "An entire new world opened up to me little by little."

Their love shaped much of her later vision of life. As she wrote in 1948:

> That most people in America look upon love as an illusion would seem to be evidenced by the many divorces we see today—and the sensuality of despair that exists all around us. But all these divorces may too be an evidence about love. They hear very little of it in this war-torn world, and they are all seeking it. Pascal said of love, "You would not seek me if you had not already found me." Just so much faith is there at any rate. A faith in love, a seeking for love. It is something then to build on, amongst the mass of people who have lost God, who do not know in what they believe tho they believe and seek for love.[10]

Forster made gauges, and Dorothy wrote articles on gardens for the Staten Island paper, a few serial stories, and the occasional feature for a socialist paper. They enjoyed the company of radical friends, the bounty of the sea, and each other. It was, she would recall later, an idyllic life, and she attributed much of her joy to Forster. "I have always felt that it was life with him that brought me natural happiness, that brought me to God," she wrote in *The Long Loneliness*.[11]

Nevertheless, she was not blind to Forster's oddities and faults. She commented: "He worked as little as possible, he shared in all the expenses of the house, but he never spent any money if he could help it. He hated social life and fled from it, and seemed afraid of any actual contact with the world, but he was much engrossed in its concerns."[12]

And yet she loved him, deeply, passionately.

I loved him in every way, as a wife, as a mother even. I loved him for all he knew and pitied him for all he didn't know. I loved him for the odds and ends I had to fish out of his sweater pockets and for the sand and shells he brought in with his fishing. I loved his lean cold body as he got into bed smelling of the sea, and I loved his integrity and stubborn pride.[13]

With Forster, Dorothy found a peace that had eluded her and a love that was based on more than mere physical attraction.

The more she fell in love, the more she heard the Hound sniffing at her heels. "Because I was grateful for love, I was grateful for life, and living with Forster made me appreciate it and even reverence it still more. He had introduced me to so much that was beautiful and good that I felt I owed to him too this renewed interest in the things of the spirit."[14]

For the Love of God

The interest she had in God and the divine that she had known in her childhood had been revived, not yet quite conventionally, but with a richness that startled her. The Hound of Heaven had her almost within his teeth.

> I was surprised that I found myself beginning to pray daily. I could not get down on my knees, but I could pray while I was walking. If I got down on my knees I thought, "Do I really believe? Whom am I praying to?" A terrible doubt came over me, and a sense of shame.... I thought suddenly scornfully, "Here you are in a stupor of content. You are biological. Like a cow. Prayer with you is like the opiate of the people." ... "But," I reasoned with myself, "I am praying because I am happy, not because I am unhappy." ... And encouraged that I was praying because I wanted to thank Him, I went on praying.[15]

Dorothy had good reason to be happy. After many years of believing that her abortion had left her sterile, she was now pregnant with Forster's child.

It was the fulfillment of her greatest desire.

FIVE

A Child Is Born

Dorothy had grieved tremendously over what she thought was sterility caused by her abortion and so was overjoyed at the prospect of being a mother.

> For a long time I had thought that I could not bear a child. A book I read years ago in school, *Silas Marner*, expressed the sorrow of a mother bereft of her child, and it expressed, too, my sorrow at my childless state. Just a few months ago I read it again, with a longing in my heart for a baby. My home, I felt, was not a home without one. The simple joys of the kitchen and garden and beach brought sadness with them because I had not the companionship of a child. No matter how much one is loved or one loves, that love is lonely without a child. It is incomplete.[1]

Learning that she could and indeed would become a parent left her "feeling so much in love, so settled, so secure" that at last she had found what she "was looking for."

Years later, in *The Catholic Worker* she would again write about the importance of children as an essential component of a full life:

> Economists tell us that in days of prosperity children are an economic asset. We assert that in these days of revolution, when we

Catholics must arm ourselves with the Holy Spirit to "renew the face of the earth," in this struggle, too, children are an asset and family life the most powerful and enduring form of propaganda.[2]

A Joy Found and Happiness Lost

Pregnancy was, quite literally, the hinge pin for the rest of her life. But her happiness was tinged with melancholy. Forster did not share her joy. Quite the opposite. She wrote that he did not believe in bringing children into the world, that he was obsessed by the war, and that he was afraid of responsibility. Being a rugged individualist, he felt that "he of all men should not be a father."

Despite the fact that he was quite nonplussed by the whole thing— since he most likely had believed, as had Dorothy, that she was incapable of bearing children—to his credit he apparently did not attempt to pressure her into an abortion. In any case, since Dorothy had once given up a child to hold onto a man's love, and had lost his love anyway, it is unthinkable that she would have been willing to do it again. In fact, in her later life she would often refer to the act of abortion as "genocide."

Sometime in December 1926, Dorothy and Forster moved from the beach to live with her sister in an apartment in the city and await the birth of their child. Sometime between then and March, when Tamar Teresa was born, Dorothy came to the decision that would change her life forever: She made up her mind that her daughter would be baptized a Catholic.

A Most Painful Decision

In *The Long Loneliness*, the pain of Dorothy's decision is apparent: "I knew that I was going to have my child baptized, cost what it may. I knew I was not going to have her floundering through many years as I had done, doubting and hesitating, undisciplined and amoral. I felt it was the greatest thing I could do for my child." And yet, ironically, she herself was still doubting and hesitant: "I prayed for the gift of faith. I was sure, yet not sure."[3]

The cost was so very high. Although she knew the Hound was waiting, she was, as Thompson's poem puts it, "sore adread, lest, having Him, [she] must have naught beside." In her case, this dilemma was literally true: To become Catholic, in fact to join any organized religion, would mean to lose Forster. "Forster," she concluded, "would have nothing to do with religion or with me if I embraced it." And so she delayed her decision.

She and Tamar and Forster moved back to the beach house in April when cold winds still raged, but the promise of spring was in the air. Dorothy's happiness was multiplied when her brother John, whom she had doted on in his babyhood, came to live with them. Her father and mother were living in Florida, where John Sr. was involved in building the Hialeah racetrack. Apparently her father paid Dorothy a small stipend to keep her brother.

It was a time of gentle joy for the family. Despite his initial misgivings, Forster fell in love with the baby and took great delight in her development. Dorothy reveled in motherhood, in her brother, in springtime at the beach, in her love for Forster. But always the decision to have Tamar baptized nibbled at the edges of her soul.

Forster, who seems to have been more passive than aggressive with most things, was unusually explicit on the subject. He considered baptism "a mumbo jumbo, the fuss and flurry peculiar to woman." The whole idea was anathema to him. The topic of religion became a wedge in their relationship, and he took to spending more and more time away from the family.

Despite her anguish, Dorothy was resolute. Tamar would be baptized, but since she didn't know any Catholics, she was uncertain how to proceed with her resolve. Then one day, she encountered Sr. Aloysia, a nun who helped take care of unwed mothers and their babies at St. Joseph's Home, a few blocks from Dorothy's beach house. With the suddenness of decision which marked her entire life, she asked how to have her baby baptized.

Sr. Aloysia might have deterred a less determined woman. She took it upon herself to teach Dorothy her catechism, but there was nothing kind, gentle, or persuasive about her approach. She expected Dorothy to memorize her lessons and recite them verbatim. If Dorothy stumbled or faltered, she received a withering tongue-lashing.

Nor were Dorothy's housekeeping and mothering techniques spared. Sr. Aloysia criticized the dirty dishes and the wood smoke on the ceiling. She made no bones about her perception that Tamar was in dire danger of death before she could be baptized.

Years later, however, Dorothy remembered Sr. Aloysia with fondness:

She was a dear, God rest her soul, and what would I have done without her!... Nothing daunted her, neither my Communist friends, nor my purely atheist friends, some of whom lived on the beach too, all close friends who observed the progress of my conversion with interest.... Dear Sisters of Charity, dear Sister Aloysia, how grateful I always will be to you![4]

Dorothy eventually did pass Sr. Aloysia's muster, and Tamar was received into the Church in July.

Forster naturally refused to attend, but he did provide lobsters for the feast that followed. Sometime during the celebration, he realized "the end to which it all portended," and he left, not to return for several days. He realized, even if Dorothy did not yet, that she was too far down the road to Rome ever to turn back.

Struggling With God

Sometimes, in reading biographies of the saints, we may conclude that holy men and women have little or no struggle once they have decided to choose God. Not so with Dorothy. She would decide to be baptized, then vacillate, then reconsider.

Her first problem was her radical social beliefs. She admitted that if she could have continued believing that communism was the answer to her desire for a cause, she would have remained a communist. In fact, she even said that in thinking about becoming a Catholic, she felt she was betraying "the class to which I belonged, the workers, the poor of the world, with whom Christ spent His life." She continued to write for socialist papers, but she was growing increasingly convinced that only faith in Christ would give true meaning to her life.

The second—and more serious—stumbling block was her love for Forster. Despite his faults, she truly loved him. "He was an anarchist and an atheist.... He was a creature of utter sincerity, and however illogical and bad-tempered about it all, I loved him. It was killing me to think of leaving him."[5]

Not only was Forster antithetical toward religion. He was also

51

vehemently antagonistic to marriage, either as a civil institution or a religious sacrament. Dorothy knew they could not continue to live together as husband and wife once she converted.

If that weren't enough, there remained the issue of her own marriage and divorce. She may have hoped that somehow Forster would change his mind, they would be civilly married, and then she would work out the details with regard to the Church later. But that was not to be.

Forster was adamant. He had always said theirs was a comradeship, not a marriage. He would not compromise his principles.

Compounding Dorothy's pain was the love Forster had for Tamar. "She was his delight," she wrote. "Which made it, of course, the harder to contemplate the cruel blow I was going to strike him when I became Catholic."[6]

Little wonder she put off her decision, instead concentrating on her daily activities and letting God work out the timing. One wonders whether years later she was thinking of her own slow journey to faith as much as her work among the poor when she wrote in *House of Hospitality*:

Do what comes to hand. Whatsoever thy hand finds to do, do it with all thy might. After all, God is with us. It shows too much conceit to trust to ourselves, to be discouraged at what we ourselves can accomplish. It is lacking in faith in God to be discouraged. After all, we are going to proceed with His help. We offer Him what we are going to do. If He wishes it to prosper, it will. We must depend solely on Him.[7]

She and Forster came and went, separated and rejoined, over the course of more than a year.

A critical juncture seems to have arrived when Nicola Sacco and Bartolomeo Vanzetti were executed for anarchism.[8] She wrote:

> Forster was stricken over the tragedy. He had always been more an anarchist than anything else in his philosophy, and so was closer to these two men than to Communist friends. He sat around the house in a stupor of misery, sickened by the cruelty of life and men. He had always taken refuge in nature as being more kindly, more beautiful and peaceful than the world of men. Now he could not even escape through nature, as he tried to escape so many problems in life.[9]

Ironically, the same event that undid Forster was a step for Dorothy toward understanding the very nature of Church. "All the nation mourned ... made up of the poor, the worker, the trade unionist—those who felt most keenly the sense of solidarity which made me gradually understand the doctrine of the Mystical Body of Christ whereby we are the members one of another."[10]

The Die Is Cast

The strain of the deteriorating relationship with Forster took its toll on Dorothy. Although she was leery of doctors, she went to the Cornell clinic, where she was diagnosed with a nervous condition. Finally, after one particularly explosive incident, she refused to let Forster back in the house.

It got to the point where it was the simple question of whether I chose God or man. I had known enough of love to know that a good healthy family life was as near to heaven as one could get in this life. There was another sample of heaven, of the enjoyment of God. The very sexual act itself was used again and again in Scripture as a figure of the beatific vision. It was not because I was tired of sex, satiated, disillusioned, that I turned to God. Radical friends used to insinuate this. It was because through whole love, both physical and spiritual, that I came to know God.[11]

The day after she turned Forster away, she left Tamar with her sister, called a priest, and arranged to be baptized.

The time had come. The Hound had treed his prey.

SIX

THE COST OF CONVERSION

Three days after Christmas 1928, Dorothy Day officially joined the Roman Catholic Church with a conditional baptism, since she had been baptized before in the Episcopal Church. It would make a nice story to say that her conversion was marked with inner peace and radiant joy, but that would be patently false.

> It was ... a most miserable day, and the trip was long from the city down to Tottenville, Staten Island. All the way on the ferry through the foggy bay I felt grimly that I was being too precipitate. I had no sense of peace, no joy, no conviction even that what I was doing was right. It was just something that I had to do, a task to be gotten through. I doubted myself when I allowed myself to think. I hated myself for being weak and vacillating. A most consuming restlessness was upon me so that I walked around and around the deck of the ferry, almost groaning in anguish of spirit.[1]

If she was uncomfortable in her decision, there was no consolation in her actions, either. At her first Communion, she went up to the Communion rail too early and had to kneel in embarrassment through the entire consecration. Nothing about the day seemed to affirm her painful choice. "I was a Catholic at last though at that

55

moment I never felt less the joy and peace and consolation which I know from my own later experiences religion can bring."[2]

Surrendering to the Hound

Why then did she enter the Church? Many people convert because of the richness of the liturgy and the grace of the sacraments, but it was quite the opposite for Dorothy.

I had no particular joy in partaking of these three sacraments, Baptism, Penance, and Holy Eucharist. I proceeded about my own active participation in them grimly, coldly, making acts of faith, and certainly with no consolation whatever. One part of my mind stood at one side and kept saying, "What are you doing? Are you sure of yourself? What kind of affectation is this? What act is this you are going through? Are you trying to induce emotion, induce faith, partake of an opiate, the opiate of the people?" I felt like a hypocrite if I got down on my knees, and shuddered at the thought of anyone seeing me.[3]

Nor was it because she recognized the fullness of truth in the Church's teaching on social justice.

I knew nothing of the social teaching of the Church at that time. I had never heard of the encyclicals. I felt that the Church was the Church of the poor, that St. Patrick's had been built from the pennies of servant girls, that it cared for emigrants, it established hospitals, orphanages, houses of the Good Shepherd, homes for the aged, but at the same time, I felt that it did not set its face against a social order which made so much charity in the present sense of the word necessary. I felt that charity was a word to choke over. Who wanted charity? And it was not just human pride but a strong sense of man's dignity and worth, and what was due him in justice, that made me resent, rather than feel proud of so mighty a sum of Catholic institutions.[4]

Nor was it the influence of some good and holy cleric or teacher that set her face toward Rome. "It was ever in my mind that human frailties and the sins and ignorances of those in high places throughout history only proved that the Church *must* be divine to have persisted through the centuries. I would not blame the Church for what I felt were the mistakes of churchmen."[5]

Nor did she enter the Church for the sake of the Church itself. Near the end of her life, she was still a bit at odds with the structure.

When I see the church taking the side of the powerful and forgetting the weak, and when I see bishops living in luxury and the poor being ignored or thrown crumbs, I know that Jesus is being insulted, as He once was, and sent to his death, as He once was. The church doesn't only belong to officials and bureaucrats; it belongs to all its people, and most especially its most humble men and women and children, the ones He would have wanted to see and help, Jesus Christ. I am embarrassed—I am *sickened*—when I see Catholics using their religion as a social ornament.[6]

She did not join the Catholic Church because of its stance on social justice, nor the richness of the liturgy, nor the example of its members. She joined for one reason only—her profound and intimate relationship with Christ and her conviction that the Church was his body here on earth. She would later write:

> I love the Church for Christ made visible. Not for itself, because it was so often a scandal to me. Romano Guardini said the Church is the Cross on which Christ was crucified; one could not separate Christ from His Cross, and one must live in a state of permanent dissatisfaction with the Church.[7]

The Never-Ending Struggle

In what may have been a bit of literary license, Dorothy recalled: "I never regretted for one minute the step which I had taken in becoming Catholic." It's hard to imagine that at least once in what she called a time of "struggle" and "little joy" she did not wonder what her life would have been like if she had not surrendered to the Hound. The only hint she gave was saying that she often began her days with weeping and sadness, a sadness that stemmed as likely as not from her longing for Forster.

If her radical, socialist beliefs were the impetus for her life's work, giving up Forster Batterham in order to join the Catholic Church was the foundation of much of her later ideology. One cannot understand the Dorothy Day who is perhaps America's premier Catholic champion of the poor without first appreciating the great personal sacrifice she endured to cast her lot with the Catholic faith. She had surrendered nothing less than everything she loved as a woman for the sake of the highest good, and she expected others to do the same.

If there is evident in Dorothy's later writing a certain intolerance and impatience with those who cannot or will not make a whole-hearted commitment to living out the demands of the Church, it is because she believed that since she had made the ultimate sacrifice, others should be able to do the same. Her decision colored her later convictions about everything from marriage and divorce to premarital sex and homosexuality.

In her column in *The Catholic Worker*, nearly thirty years after her conversion, Dorothy's sense of sacrifice was still evident: "Neither revolutions nor faith are won without keen suffering. For me Christ was not to be bought for thirty pieces of silver but with my heart's blood. We buy not cheap in this market." [8]

Her conviction that one can choose to do the right thing, no matter what the personal cost, was rooted in her own experience. She was not immune to the temptations of the body, but she firmly believed that with the aid of prayer, the sacraments—especially Confession—and a determined effort, one could rise above sinful nature to resurrection with Christ. After all, that's what she had done, and she did not consider herself particularly heroic or saintly.

A Love Without End

Dorothy continued to love Forster all the rest of her life. Celibacy was not a natural virtue for her. She wrote (in decidedly non-feminist terms) in *The Long Loneliness*:

A woman does not feel whole without a man. And for a woman who had known the joys of marriage, yes, it was hard. It was years before I awakened without that longing for a face pressed against my breast, an arm about my shoulders. The sense of loss was there. It was a price I had paid. I was Abraham who had sacrificed Isaac.[9]

For the rest of her life, she would suffer from bouts of profound loneliness, and it was only her faith that kept her from despair.

One time ... I was traveling, far from home and lonely, and I awoke in the night almost on the verge of weeping with a sense of futility, of being unloved and unwanted. And suddenly the thought came to me of my importance as a daughter of God, daughter of a King, and I felt a sureness of God's love and at the same time a conviction that one of the greatest injustices (if one can put it that way) which one can do to God is to distrust His love, not realize His love.[10]

As late as 1967, she would still say, "I had to give up a common-law husband with whom I was very much in love and with whom I still feel a most loving friendship."

She expressed that love in concrete terms one last time in the fall of 1959. Shortly after Dorothy had left him, Forster had taken another common-law-wife, Nanette. Thirty years later, she was dying of cancer, and in his grief, Forster turned to Dorothy and his sister Lily, who had introduced them so many years before.

Dorothy and Lily spent the next few months helping to nurse Nanette. Dorothy was there at the deathbed when Nanette asked to be baptized. True to form to the end, Forster rejected any notion of religion at the funeral home. He simply wanted Nanette cremated, because "this is the end. I want no praying over her," Dorothy recalled him saying.

Although she did not speak directly about it, her reflections on the joys of family life hint that she never forgot the pain she had caused Forster by removing him from his daughter nor the challenges of raising a girl without a father. For instance, she wrote: "This day, for the sake of the family, there are so many compromises. But we must learn to accept this hardest of all sufferings, the suffering of those nearest and dearest to us. Thank God for this training in suffering."[11]

Following Through

Dorothy was nothing if not determined. Having made her decision to become Catholic, she would live with the consequences, come what may. Grimly, she went to Mass and Confession, said her prayers, and prepared for Confirmation under the tutelage of a Fr. Zachary, who gave her a book of meditations and a *St. Andrew's Missal.*

With the exception of the absence of Forster and her increased participation in church activities, Dorothy's immediate post-baptism life wasn't all that different from her pre-baptism life. She and Tamar moved back to the city for the rest of the winter, where she supported them by synopsizing novels for MGM and handing out publicity with the communist-affiliated Anti-Imperialist league. She kept the job with the communists on the advice of Fr. Zachary, who, being a practical man, told her not to let it go until she could find another one.

And so she continued until, a year after her baptism, on the feast of

Pentecost, she was confirmed under the name Maria Teresa with a large group of other adults at the Convent of the Holy Souls. She finally found the peace that she had sought in vain her since her baptism. "My confirmation was indeed joyful," she later wrote, "and Pentecost never passes without a renewed sense of happiness and thanksgiving. It was only then that the feeling of uncertainty finally left me, never again to return, praise God!"[12]

But one restlessness resolved soon gave way to another rediscovered. Joining the Church did not mean she had abandoned her radical convictions. But she found it difficult to express them within the context of her new faith.

The next few years were particularly itinerant for Dorothy. She returned to California to work for a movie studio but found Hollywood trite and boring, so she left at the end of her three-month contract. She and Tamar then sojourned in Mexico, which Dorothy found more to her liking, returning to New York only because Tamar fell ill. She may have spent some time in Florida with her parents as well.

Continuing to attend daily Mass and make frequent Confession, Dorothy gradually gave up her former life and friends. "After I had become a Catholic," she said, "I began little by little to lose track of my friends. Being a Catholic, I discovered, put a barrier between me and others; however slight, it was always felt." She knew few Catholics, commenting that she "did not know personally one Catholic layman" and had no real idea how she was going to live now that she had thrown her lot in with the Church of Rome.

A Most Fateful Day

All of that changed one fateful day in November 1932. Dorothy had been writing more or less regularly for the Catholic magazine *Commonweal* and proposed to cover a "Hunger March" that was being held in Washington, D.C. The Jesuit weekly *America* agreed to pay her to report on a farmers' convention that was being held at the same time. So she and another journalist friend from her days of writing for *The Masses*, Mary Heaton Vorse, attended the December 8 parade.

She experienced conflicting emotions:

> I stood on the curb and watched them, joy and pride in the courage of this band of men and women mounting in my heart, and with it a bitterness too that since I was now a Catholic, with fundamental philosophical differences, I could not be out there with them. I could write, I could protest, to arouse the conscience, but where was the Catholic leadership in the gathering of bands of men and women together, for the actual works of mercy that the comrades had always made part of their technique in reaching the workers?
>
> How little, how puny my work had been since becoming a Catholic, I thought. How self-centered, how ingrown, how lacking in sense of community![13]

When the demonstration was over and she had met her reporting deadline, she went to the National Shrine at Catholic University on the feast of the Immaculate Conception. There she poured out her heart: "I offered up a special prayer, a prayer which came with tears and with anguish that some way would open up for me to use what I possessed for my fellow workers, for the poor."[14]

She got her answer in the form of an odd little French peasant by the name of Peter Maurin.

SEVEN

An Unlikely Mentor

It is impossible to talk about the rest of Dorothy's life without first discussing Peter Maurin (anglicized to "Maw-rin" despite his French background). The man she called "a genius, a saint, an agitator, a writer, a lecturer, a poor man, and a shabby tramp, all in one" gave her lofty idealism an earthly platform. His spirit and ideas dominated the rest of her life and permeated her work. It was one of her greatest disappointments that her three-hundred-page manuscript on Peter and his principles never found a publisher.

Through Peter Maurin's influence, Dorothy came to an understanding of what he (and she) called a synthesis of "cult, culture, and cultivation." For the rest of her life, she never tired of talking or writing about Peter. As her biographer William Miller said, "What Peter Maurin did for Dorothy was to reorient her vision from the object to the subject, from collectivism to Christian personalism. He also provided her with something she had not had—an understanding of the meaning of the Church and her position in it."[1]

Peter Maurin

Peter Maurin was one of twenty-three children born to a French peasant family living two hundred miles from Barcelona at the turn of the last century. After working at various jobs, including cocoa salesman, and spending some time as a Christian Brother, he went to homestead in Canada. When his partner was killed, he wandered about, eventually ending up in the States.

As Dorothy put it:

He worked on farms, in brickyards, in steel mills, at every kind of unskilled labor, from Chicago to New York. He settled in Chicago for a time and gave French lessons, using the methods, so I understand, of the Berlitz School, and was successful at it. He read constantly, he worked, and he taught. He was always the teacher. When he could not get people to listen, he wrote out his ideas in neat, lettered script, duplicated the leaflets, and distributed them himself on street corners, an undignified apostolate.[2]

Immediately before meeting Dorothy, Peter had worked at a boys' camp in New York state, mending roads, cutting ice, and living with the horse in the barn. During the camp's off season, he would come to the city to preach his message in Union Square, living in absolute poverty. Although he advised people to beg if they were in need, he himself preferred to go without.

Dorothy wrote:

He never refused to give alms, no matter how poor he was. He believed in poverty and loved it and felt it a liberating force. He differentiated between poverty and destitution, but the two often came close together in his life, when to give to others he had to strip himself. He never had more than the clothes on his back, but he took the Gospel counsel literally.... That is, if he encountered anyone needing a coat, and he had already given his own away, he would take the person to some friend and ask for a coat for him.[3]

A devout Catholic with a devotion to the Mass and the Eucharist, Peter was peculiar to the point of oddness. Whereas others were put off by his appearance and odor (he seldom bathed), Dorothy saw beyond the externals. For her, Peter Maurin represented everything she believed we are called to be as Catholics. He was

... a pilgrim and stranger on earth, using the things of the world as though he used them not, availing himself of only what he needed and discarding all excess baggage. I think of him walking down the street slowly, leisurely, deep in thought, his hands clasped behind him. He paid no attention whatever to traffic lights; I suppose he put his faith in his guardian angel.[4]

Despite their outward differences, Peter shared similarities with the two men Dorothy had loved before her conversion, Moise and Forster. All were loners, with notable disdain for convention. Self-centered individualists, they displayed their emotional wounds without pretense of social bandage. Eccentric, intellectual, and passionate for their causes, they stimulated Dorothy intellectually as much as they stirred her desire to nurture and care.

Dorothy was not blind to their faults, but she seems to have loved all three *because of*—not despite—their failings. By the time she met Peter, however, Dorothy was able to distinguish eros from agape. Her love for Peter, far from being rooted in romantic attachment, was based entirely on her passion for the Hound of Heaven.

"A St. Benedict Joseph Labré"

While readily admitting her admiration for Peter and the debt she felt she owed him for helping her discover her life's purpose, Dorothy also confessed that she found him difficult to take at times. Not only did he read continually to her; he pestered her nonstop with comments on what he had read. She was short with him at times, although he never seemed to notice the rebukes, so wrapped up was he in his own thoughts.

I was sure of Peter—sure that he was a saint and a great teacher—although, to be perfectly honest, I wondered if I really liked Peter sometimes. He was twenty years older than I, he spoke with an accent so thick it was hard to penetrate to the thought beneath, he had a one-track mind, he did not like music, he did not read Dickens or Dostoevsky, and he did not bathe.

In the summer when he was ill, there were times when it was hard to be in the same room with him. Only when he was old and sick could we put him under the shower every Saturday and change his clothes and bedding and look after him as he should be looked after. I am sensitive about writing these things, but I feel I must point out that it was no natural "liking" that made me hold Peter in reverent esteem and gave me confidence that all I learned from him was sound and the program he laid down for us was the right one for our time.

If Peter resembled a St. Benedict Joseph Labré, that too was a lesson for the rest of us, who spend so much time keeping, cleaning, changing, and looking after our clothes, taking care of the perishable body to the neglect of mind and soul.[5]

The Initial Encounter

Dorothy always believed that their first meeting was a direct answer to prayer. She had just returned from her emotion-filled trip to the Washington Hunger March. There she had seen clearly for the first time the abyss separating her from her former life that her conversion had created—the distance her faith would force her to take from her earlier worldview.

She had poured her heart out in prayer at the National Cathedral and had ridden a bus for eight hours. All she wanted to do was see Tamar, her brother John, and his wife, Tessa, who had been baby-sitting. She needed only to find a little "quiet and cup of coffee."

Instead, she discovered a short, stocky man in his mid-fifties, "as ragged and rugged as any of the marchers [she] had left," patiently waiting for her. He introduced himself simply—"I am Peter Maurin"—then added: "George Shuster, editor of the *Commonweal*, told me to look you up. Also, a red-headed Irish Communist in Union Square told me to see you. He says we think alike." With that as a preamble, he launched into a lengthy discourse, oblivious to Dorothy's fatigue and dismay.

It was typical of Peter's impractical approach to life to seek her without so much as an address. It was just as typical of God's help that he found her. He simply began asking people in New York if they had heard of her. When he bumped into the red-haired communist in Union Square, he learned where Dorothy lived and arrived on her doorstep, confident she would welcome him and be prepared to talk all night about his ideas. Dorothy was not impressed.

[He] started talking at once—casually, informally, almost as though he were taking up a conversation where it had been left off. There was a grey look about him: he had grey hair, cut short and scrubby; grey eyes; strong features; a pleasant mouth; and short-fingered, broad hands, evidently used to heavy work, such as with a pick and shovel. He wore the kind of old clothes that have so lost their shape and finish that it's impossible to tell whether they are clean or not.[6]

Easy Essays

Dorothy recalled how that day Peter recited one of his own unique syntheses of thought, which her brother John dubbed "Easy Essays."

People go to Washington
Asking the government
To solve their economic problems,
To solve men's economic problems.
Thomas Jefferson says that
The less government there is
The better it is.
If the less government there is,
The better it is,
Then the best kind of government
Is self-government.
If the best kind of government
Is self-government,
Then the best kind of organization

Is self-organization.
When the organizers try
To organize the unorganized,
Then the organizers
Don't organize themselves.
And when the organizers
Don't organize themselves,
Nobody organizes himself,
And when nobody organizes himself
Nothing is organized.[7]

Dorothy didn't have much time or inclination to listen right then, since Tamar had the measles and the doctor had been summoned. Peter didn't care. He just kept talking—to the doctor, the plumber, the gas man, Tess, John.

In fact, he had been to Dorothy's place before, while she was in Washington, and because he had missed her then, he was doubly anxious to meet her and get started on what he called his "indoctrinations." It was only because of the innate hospitality of her sister-in-law Tess that he was allowed back after his initial visit. "My brother was a conventional American," Dorothy said, "and Peter often gave the impression of being a dangerous and unbalanced radical when he began 'indoctrinating' someone who was unprepared."

Having dispensed with all introductions and ignored the conventions of small talk, he probably would have expounded all night on his ideas for a new social order if the totally exhausted Dorothy hadn't shooed him out the door. Undaunted, he returned the next day and began to educate her on the history of the Church and the great thinkers of the century, such as Mauriac, Maritain, Péguy, and the encyclicals of the popes—as well as his own ideas of how to build a new society, based entirely on Christian principles and emphasizing the need for hospitality. He explained it this way:

Houses of Hospitality

1. We need Houses of Hospitality
   to give to the rich
   the opportunity
   to serve the poor.
2. We need Houses of Hospitality
   to bring the scholars
   to the workers
   or the workers
   to the scholars.
3. We need Houses of Hospitality
   to bring back to institutions
   the technique to institutions.
4. We need Houses of Hospitality
   to show
   what idealism looks like
   when it is practiced.[8]

Peter had chosen Dorothy to be his disciple because he had read articles she had written in Catholic magazines. As she put it: "[He] had come to suggest I start a newspaper to bring about 'clarification of thought.' Clarification was the first 'point' in his program."[9]

Clarification of Thought

Peter's primary method of clarifying was to talk ... and talk ... and talk. Once Dorothy compared him to St. Paul, who was reported to have spoken so long that a young man drifted off to sleep, fell out of an open window, and was picked up for dead. Peter considered himself to be a teacher par excellence, but his only teaching aids were his forefinger, which he jabbed in the air to punctuate his points and notes, either from books he had read or in his own script.

"His pockets are full of pamphlets, pages torn from books," Dorothy later said. "He tears pages from them ruthlessly—those pages which illustrate his ideas—and he brings them out to enforce his points." What Dorothy did not say was that the books he so blithely mangled were generally hers.

Peter must have been a thoroughly annoying person. Dorothy said that no matter what she was doing, whether housework or shopping or tending to Tamar, Peter was at her side talking incessantly. She would beg for a breather, to no avail. Once when she and Tessa were trying to listen to a symphony on the radio (she thinks it was Tchaikovsky's *Pathétique*), she got him to be quiet for a little while. But before long:

> His face started working, his eyes lit up, his nose twitched, his finger began to mark out points in the air before him. Usually he'd take out a notebook and start jotting down points. Finally, when he could bear it no longer, he looked at me wistful and then, seeing my adamant expression, turned to Tess. I remember that night especially because he went over and knelt down by her chair and began whispering to her, unable to restrain himself longer.[10]

At first Dorothy didn't really grasp what he was saying:

> It was a long time before I really knew what Peter was talking
> about that first day. But he did make three points I thought I
> understood: founding a newspaper for clarification of thought,
> starting houses of hospitality, and organizing farming com-
> munes. I did not really think then of the latter two as having
> anything to do with me, but I did know about newspapers.[11]

The Catholic Worker

Being practical as well as idealistic, Dorothy quizzed Peter on how to
publish a paper without money. "In the Catholic Church one never
needs any money to start a good work," Peter replied. "People are what
are important. If you have the people and they are willing to give their
work—that is the thing. God is not to be outdone in generosity. The
funds will come in somehow or other."

In her history of the Catholic Worker movement, *Loaves and Fishes*,
Dorothy wonders, "Did he really say this? I cannot be sure now, and I
suspect that he passed over my question about money—it was not
needed in the Church. The important thing was work."

Dorothy had been reading the life of Rose Hawthorne Lathrop, the
daughter of novelist Nathaniel Hawthorne, who founded a cancer
hospital that grew into a new order of Dominican sisters. Thus she was
already inspired to start her own good work. Moreover:

> The appearance of Peter Maurin, I felt with deep conviction,
> was the result of my prayers. Just as the good God had used the

farmer Habakkuk to bring the mess of food intended for the reapers to Daniel in the lions' den, so had He sent Peter Maurin to bring me the good intellectual food I needed to strengthen me to work for Him.[12]

She had a typewriter, a kitchen table, paper, and enthusiasm. *The Catholic Worker* was underway.

EIGHT

WORK FOR THE WORKER

Picas and bylines flowed in Dorothy's veins, as they had in her father's and as they did in her brothers', both of whom worked for more conventional newspapers. Journalism was her occupation. Now it would be her vocation as well.

While some of Peter's more arcane points escaped her, her passion was ignited by the idea of a newspaper in which she could express her ideas and motivate the masses of Catholics to bring about the kingdom of God as understood by the Catholic faith. This, she felt, was what she was born to do. But how would they begin such an endeavor? she asked Peter.

Starting at the Beginning

He had no idea. "I enunciate the principles," he declared loftily. (One can imagine her frustration at such a remark!) His only practical suggestion was to recommend she contact a priest friend of his in a large parish to see whether they could use his mimeograph machine to run off some copies.

Dorothy soon dismissed that as a pipe dream. Looking for a more realistic avenue, she approached Paulist Press and learned that she could get twenty-five hundred copies of an eight-page, tabloid-sized paper printed for fifty-seven dollars.

She worried that her electricity and gas would be turned off, and she and Tamar would be forced on the streets, because her own bills would be unpaid. Nevertheless, she decided to publish the paper using her own money. She had fifteen dollars coming from an article for *Sign* magazine; she had some money due from a research job and a couple of other articles she had written. Sr. Peter Claver, who would become a lifelong friend, gave her a dollar, and a Father Ahearn, pastor of a Newark parish, gave her ten dollars.

It was all she needed. She made the commitment both mentally and financially. Almost literally "on the wings of prayer," an important chapter in both advocacy journalism and the American Catholic Church was begun.

Somehow by the grace of God and the intercession of St. Joseph, her favorite patron, Dorothy's own bills were paid. She was not evicted, although to pay for the printing of the second issue she had to sell her typewriter—something she did not necessarily do with gladness. She wrote years later in her regular column: "We all hold on—to our books, our tools such as typewriters, our clothes; and instead of rejoicing when they are taken from us, we lament."[1]

Catholic Radicals Start *The Catholic Worker*

The first issue came out on May Day, 1933. Dorothy decided that the paper would be called *The Catholic Worker*—she envisioned its becoming the Catholic response to the Communist paper *The Daily Worker*. Peter wanted it named *The Catholic Radical,* but Dorothy's decision prevailed, whether, as she said, Peter demurred or, as is equally likely, she insisted. In any event, *The Catholic Worker* it was, and *The Catholic Worker* it would remain.

Its purpose was clear from the beginning:

To Our Readers

For those who are sitting on park benches in the warm spring sunlight.

For those who are huddling in shelters trying to escape the rain.

For those who are walking the streets in the all but futile search for work.

For those who think that there is no hope for the future, no recognition of their plight—this little paper is addressed.

It is printed to call their attention to the fact that the Catholic Church has a social program—to let them know that there are men of God who are working not only for their spiritual, but their material welfare.[2]

What made *The Catholic Worker* unique in the annals of Catholic journalism was its blend of orthodox Catholic teaching with its demand for radical social change. Without official ties to the Church and yet intimately interwoven with the faith, *The Catholic Worker* stands as a monument to lay vision and lay apostolates. In many ways, it paved the way for reception of the social teachings of the bishops, later writings of the popes, and Vatican II itself.

The first editorial clarified Dorothy and Peter's passion:

It's time there was a Catholic paper printed for the unemployed.

The fundamental aim of most radical sheets is the conversion of its readers to radicalism and atheism.

Is it not possible to be radical and not atheist?

Is it not possible to protest, to expose, to complain, to point out abuses and demand reforms without desiring the overthrow of religion?

In an attempt to popularize and make known the encyclicals of the Popes in regard to social justice and the program put forth by the Church, for the "reconstruction of the social order," this news sheet, *The Catholic Worker*, is started.[3]

Not What Was Expected

As the paper was being assembled, Peter grew increasingly discontent. He made it clear that what he had envisioned was not a radical newspaper in the classic sense—with news reports on the plight of Southern blacks and sharecroppers, child labor, and striking workers, along with editorials—but a mouth organ for his ideas. He assumed Dorothy would print nothing but his own "Easy Essays," eight full pages of his syntheses of Catholic thought and inspiration.

When the proof pages for the first edition came, he could take no more. "It's everyone's paper," he said. "And everyone's paper is no one's paper." He walked out the door without a word, returning to the boys' camp in upstate New York where he had worked before he met Dorothy.

Dorothy might have admired Peter. She might have thought him "a saint," as she later said. She might have believed he was her direct answer to prayer. But she was the journalist, and it was *her* newspaper. For the rest of her life, it might as well have been called *Dorothy Day's Catholic Worker.*

Despite her sadness over Peter's departure and her sincere wish that he would be present when the first copies were sold on Union Square, she didn't change the content. "His absence gave me an uneasy feeling, reminding me that our paper was not reflecting his thought, although it was he who had given us the idea," she wrote. But she added with characteristic brusqueness: "Then, for a while I was too busy again to think much about it."[4]

In order to get a second class mailing permit, the paper had to be sold rather than given away, so Dorothy decided to charge a penny a copy—"the least possible price on it to indicate how you feel about money."

The Adventure Begins

May 1, 1933, was historic for many reasons. The Soviets were celebrating their most massive May Day ever. In Germany, the first "labor day" of the Third Reich was organized. In New York, as many as fifty thousand gathered in Union Square to foment social change. Dorothy and three helpers plunged into the crowds to preach their own unique brand of revolution based entirely on the gospel of Jesus Christ and to sell their inchoate newspaper.

It was an ignominious start. No converts were made, and few copies of the paper were purchased, but Dorothy was undaunted. She sent out *The Catholic Worker* to anyone she thought would read it and made it clear that a donation would not be unwelcome.

She continued to work more or less alone, until a few weeks later, Peter strolled back into her life as if he had never been gone, pulled out some notes, and began his incessant indoctrination. He never explained why he had left, saying only, "Man proposes and woman disposes."

At their first meeting, Peter had told Dorothy he saw her as a Catherine of Siena "who would move mountains and have influence on governments, temporal and spiritual."[5] (He didn't add that he saw this happening through the promulgation of his ideas and his ideas only!) Now, however, he no longer saw her as being enlightened by the Holy Spirit, "but as an ex-Socialist, ex-I.W.W., ex-Communist, in whom he might find some concordance, some basis on which to build."[6] Ironically, history would witness that his initial assessment was closer to the truth than his latter.

If he had hoped to change Dorothy's mind on the content of the newspaper, he had underestimated his protégée. The issues that had enflamed her as a communist would continue to stir her as a Christian. "The bottle will still smell of the liquor it once held," she commented. To her dying day, whiffs of socialism, communism, and revolution could always be caught in her writing.

The second issue of the newspaper did contain Peter's editorial calling for, among other things, the establishment of Houses of Hospitality:

In the Middle Ages, it was an obligation of the bishop to provide houses of hospitality or hospices for the wayfarer. They are especially necessary now and necessary to my program, as halfway houses. I am hoping that someone will donate a house rent-fee for six months so that a start may be made. A priest will be at the head of it and men gathered from our round-table discussions [another favorite idea of his] will be recruited to work in the houses cooperatively and eventually sent out to farm colonies or agronomic universities.[7]

It was not even the lead editorial. "Perhaps it sounded too utopian for my tastes," Dorothy recalls. More likely it was because she "was irked because women were left out in his description of a house of hospitality, where he spoke of a group of men living under a priest."[8]

Surprised by Success

The Catholic Worker launched at one of the bleakest times in American history. The Great Depression held the nation by its throat, and unemployment was rampant. The message of hope that *The Catholic Worker* offered was welcomed by those who longed for a better world, but who found the secularism of communism unfulfilling.

Six months after its inception, the paper's circulation was 20,000. At its peak in 1940, it reached more than 120,000. Even Dorothy was a bit surprised by its success.

We got letters from all parts of the country from people who said they had picked up the paper on trains, in rooming houses. One letter came from the state of Sonora in Mexico and we read with amazement that the reader had tossed in an uncomfortable bed on a hot night until he got up to turn over the mattress and under it found a copy of *The Catholic Worker.* A miner found a copy five miles underground in an old mine that stretched out under the Atlantic Ocean off Nova Scotia. A seminarian said that he had sent out his shoes to be half-soled in Rome and they came back to him wrapped in a copy of *The Catholic Worker.*[9]

Good Catholic Journalism

The Catholic Worker, for all its not-so-hidden agenda, adhered to principles of good journalism. Dorothy believed in eyewitness reporting, not surprising since that was her stock in trade. She firmly believed that it wasn't enough to sit at a typewriter pounding out lofty words. The writer had to, in the words of a later generation, "walk the walk and talk the talk."

She once explained that her newspaper had "many writers and editors. But they [were] all so engaged in baking bread, making soup, begging from the market, not to speak of taking care of St. Joseph's House that writing [was] always done at the last minute."[10]

Not that she tolerated slap-dash efforts. Her own writing, which is extensive, shows the seeming effortlessness that comes both from natural ability and careful rewriting. Just a sample of her craft: "Our lives are made up of little miracles day by day. That splendid globe of sun, one street wide, framed at the foot of East Fourteenth Street in early-morning mists, that greeted me on my way out to Mass was a miracle that lifted up my heart."[11]

Even when writing about the grinding poverty she faced daily, she put her own deft touch on the work:

There is a smell of grapes in the air—rich, luscious Concord grapes. If this editorial has a melancholy note, it is not because chestnuts are wormy or because the stove has cracked, but because all our Italian neighbors are too poor this year to buy grapes and make wine. Grapes that used to be one dollar a box are now one dollar fifty. And the Italian fathers who love their wine and have it in lieu of fresh vegetables and fruits all during the long winter are still out of jobs or on four-day-a-month work relief and this year there is no pleasant smell of fermenting grapes, no disorderly heaps of mash dumped in the gutters.[12]

Gathering Forces

As the paper began to grow, Dorothy rented the store downstairs from her apartment for an office. By the force of her personality as much as anything, she began collecting people around her. One was Big Dan Orr, who sold the paper to make enough money to subsist.

Standing on the street corner, hawking his wares, Dan would often be in competition with men selling *The Daily Worker*. When they would shout, "Read *The Daily Worker!*" he would retort, "Read *The Catholic Worker* daily!" He rented a horse and wagon from a German Nazi to deliver the papers. To Dorothy's dismay, he would take the blanket from her bed to cover the horse in the winter. (She wasn't very fond, either, of another Catholic worker who used her washcloth to wipe his cat's face.)

Dorothy remembers the first time she and Dan met.

[He was] groaning and shouting, and, when asked what we could do for him, he bellowed, "I'd like to soak my feet!" He had been walking the streets all day, looking for a job.... I brought out a washtub of hot water. He gratefully took off his socks, which were full of holes, and gingerly, one after the other, put his feet into the hot water, roaring his delight. I was thinking of the time Jesus washed the feet of His apostles and then told them, "As I have done to you, so you do also." But I couldn't bring myself to do any more than offer the tub of hot water, soap, and towels. It would have been too embarrassing.[13]

For all her sacrifice on behalf of the poor, Dorothy found it difficult, if not almost impossible, personally to "kiss the leper" as St. Francis had done. When dealing with particularly unsavory people, she gritted her teeth, held her breath, and tried to offer it up. "I do penance through my nose continually," she once said.

She talked about twice being more or less forced into literally kissing one of the poor she served, and her revulsion was apparent. "It is not likely," she wrote, "that I shall be vouchsafed the vision of Elizabeth of Hungary who put the leper in her bed and later, going to tend him, saw no longer the leper's stricken face, but the face of Christ."[14] In these words one gets the feeling that she was as adverse to putting "lepers" in her bed as she was removed from overt signs of mysticism.

As the months went by, Peter was not satisfied with merely his talking and Dorothy's writing about change (even if he did become more or less resigned to the fact that the paper was not going to become his exclusive province). He wanted to open his Houses of Hospitality to "give the rich an opportunity to serve the poor." As usual, he was long on thought and short on practicality, jabbing his finger in the air to make his point while leaving the details to Dorothy to figure out. "We are not an organization, we are an organism," he would say.

If he considered himself the (talking) head of the organism, then Dorothy understood who it was he had designated to be its hands. And, as usual, she took matters into her capable grasp.

NINE

TOGETHER WE STAND

Peter wanted a new world order, a cross between communism—where everyone worked according to his or her means and received according to his or her need—and the earliest days of Christianity, when the believers held everything in common. The first step in ushering in this new utopia was to spread the word. *The Catholic Worker* was doing that—sort of—since it used many of his "Easy Essays," although not as many as he undoubtedly would have liked.

Houses of Hospitality

The second step in the plan was the establishment of Houses of Hospitality. Peter undoubtedly saw these houses in grand terms—places where the poor would have their dignity restored, where the rich would learn the joys of service, where the intellectuals would be fed by the wisdom of common sense and the common would be stimulated by the ideals of the intellect.

It's hard to be sure what Dorothy truly thought. She idealized Peter, blaming herself when she failed to grasp the intricacies of his vision. "What an inspired attitude Peter took in his painful and patient indoctrination—and what a small part of it we accepted."[1]

If Peter said it was important, then Dorothy believed it to be so. However, since she was left to carry out his rarified ideas in the real world, it's likely she intuited that Peter's Areopagus would become her soup kitchen. After all, she was the one getting up before dawn to work on the breadlines.

Peter, meanwhile, "was never tired, for he had already acquired the habit of staying up until two or three in the morning, or as long as a discussion lasted, and then sleeping the next morning until just in time to get up for noonday Mass."[2] Without a trace of self-pity, Dorothy threw herself into creating a House of Hospitality—if not with the same passion that she began *The Catholic Worker*, at least with a willing enthusiasm.

Humble Beginnings

The house opened in the barbershop beneath her apartment. Almost immediately Dorothy and her troop of followers began serving meals to the homeless who wandered in at all times of the day and night. And not just the homeless. Much to Peter's delight, professors and other notables he invited came to talk and to argue.

Each week a new speaker would address the small group that gathered. "The best was none too good for the poor, we thought, so we had such priests as Father La Farge, S.J., Father Joseph McSorley and Father Paul Hanly Furfey of Catholic University, not to mention such distinguished visitors as Jacques Maritain and Hilaire Belloc," Dorothy recalled.[3]

A picture taken of Jacques Maritain with Dorothy, Peter, and some of the Catholic workers shows a proud and smiling Peter and a rather dour, turtleneck-wearing Dorothy in the back. It's no wonder Peter was beaming and Dorothy was grim. His dream was being erected on her broad shoulders.

It is likely that when the picture was taken financial burdens were, as always, in the forefront of her mind. Despite the monetary implications, she was determined to dispose that which Peter proposed, but it was an ongoing stress. "Economic security," she wrote, "something every reader and we ourselves would like to have, is not for us. We must live by faith, from day to day, knowing that we have good friends in St. Joseph, St. Teresa, St. John Bosco, who lived through these same struggles themselves."[4]

The growth of the Houses of Hospitality was nothing short of amazing, matching as they did the amazing needs of the time. Soon they had an apartment for women and another place for men. Within a year they had a maternity guild and a workers' school, as well as a clothing distribution area and the original soup kitchen. Eventually they moved to a building on Mott Street, where they stayed for fourteen years, from 1936 to 1950.

At Home on Mott Street

Dorothy, being a city girl at heart, loved Mott Street. She wrote almost rapturously about it in 1936:

> The buildings are six stories high and the street narrows so that little sun shines here excepting the middle of the day. But below Grand Street the push carts begin, and these take from the drabness of the street, and the bright fruits and vegetables light up the

scene. Here are grapes, mushrooms, yellow squash, tomatoes, bananas, beans, and greens of all kinds; fish stands with whelks and live eels and snails. Here are cheese stores and cheese pressed into the shape of reindeer and pigs....

There are spaghetti stores with all variety of spaghetti, all shapes, all lengths.... There are bakeries and from down in the basements where there are ovens built in, the warm delicious smell of fresh loaves steals out into the street to mingle with the smell of pizza.[5]

Perhaps one reason she lavished so much attention on the food in the area was that, as she said, "the breadlines were not long in forming."

It is ironic that the popular image of Dorothy Day is one of her standing with a long trail of dejected-looking men snaking past her as she beatifically ladles soup and hands out bread. In truth, she hated lines and wasn't all that fond of working the breadline. Of that time, she wrote:

Having spent most of the night in heated discussion and neglecting the time, I was in no mood to crawl out at 5:30 this morning to do a turn on the breadline. But the quickest way to forget sleepiness is to roll out, wet my face and turn on the radio in the store—which I did.

It is hard to cut a mountain of bread and prepare it for serving. I say hard because it seems hours before the job is complete. The eyes of the men outside peering in keep saying—it's cold out there, or, he is about ready now.... I am relieved now to go to Mass which means I must pass a whole block of hungry, waiting men.... It is awful to think this will start again tomorrow.[6]

Characters Build Character

Along with those looking for their literal serving of daily bread were the more permanent members of the motley crew of Mott Street. Dorothy writes in *Loaves and Fishes*, her history of *The Catholic Worker*, "It sometimes seemed that the more space we had, the more people came to us for help, so that our quarters were never quite adequate. But somehow we managed. Characters of every description and from every corner of life turned up—and we welcomed them all."[7]

Characters such as Mr. Breen, an outspoken racist, who called Dorothy a "nigger lover" for helping blacks as well as whites. His attitude tried her patience sorely, since, from the very beginning of *The Catholic Worker*, no one was turned away because of skin color. Indeed, the insignia of *The Catholic Worker* showed both a black and a white worker, united in their common struggle.

Dorothy allowed Mr. Breen to remain with them until his death, trying, as she said, to give love where there was no love. It wasn't easy.

As the end drew near we all sat around his bedside, taking turns saying the rosary. In his late moments, Mr. Breen looked up at us and said,

"I have only one possession left in the world—my cane. I want you to have it. Take it—take it and wrap it around the necks of some of these bastards around here."[8]

Through such trials—and worse—Dorothy persisted, even though Peter was somewhat disappointed. "Our Houses of Hospitality are scarcely the kind of houses that Peter Maurin has envisioned in his plan for a new social order," she wrote. "He recognizes that himself and thinks in terms of the future to accomplish true centers of Catholic Action and rural centers."[9]

A Never-Changing Need

Houses of Hospitality spread through the country, all operating independently under the auspices of lay men and women. Their numbers declined after World War II, when America entered a period of prosperity and new federal legislation such as the Social Security Act changed the face of poverty. Nevertheless, even today, in the opening years of the twenty-first century, Houses of Hospitality continue to be established to serve the poor, the needy, the neglected, and the unwanted.

Dorothy's words, written at the height of the movement, remain as true today as they did then: "As we face a new threat of unemployment under the shadow of automation, as we face daily terrors of world destruction, such centers of mutual help in the spirit of brotherhood—under whatever name, or in whatever guise—were never more desperately needed than they are right now."[10]

Having been caught by the Hound of Heaven, Dorothy was now willing to run along his trail. She firmly believed he was running with the poor.

Back to the Land

While Houses of Hospitality have persisted and continue to be established, the third plank of Peter's program for social reform—communitarian farms—was far less successful. The idea sprang from his intense dislike of wage-based economics, a system in which a worker was tied to a paycheck, doing a job that might not suit his or her natural abilities, but was needed in order to purchase the necessities of life. This system gave rise to what Peter considered the abominable practice of lending money at interest, which further tethered workers to often demeaning work.

His solution was to establish farming communes where people would live out their vocations in service of the common good. Food would come from the land itself, and in a foretaste of heaven on earth, all would be able to live simple, fulfilling lives in harmony. On these "agronomic universities," as he called them, would be found "the solution to all the ills of the world: unemployment, delinquency, destitute old age, man's rootlessness, lack of room for growing families, and hunger."[11]

As usual, the responsibility for fulfilling his vision fell to Dorothy. She was, as she put it, "less than enthusiastic." She was a city girl through and through, even though she appreciated occasional sojourns in the country.

"I loved the life of the city," she wrote. "Especially I loved the life of the Lower East Side, where, in my neighborhood, every Italian back yard had its own fig tree and grape arbor."[12] But what Peter wanted, Dorothy was determined to get for him, so in the spring of 1936 they acquired an acre of land on Staten Island.

In retrospect, Dorothy's initial reluctance should have been a red flag. Despite numerous later attempts in several locations, none of the "agronomic universities" ever truly succeeded in the way Peter had envisioned. When she purchased a larger parcel of land they called Mary Farm in Easton, Pennsylvania, they should have been further warned when they discovered that the farm they bought so cheaply had no water source. The only water came from rain collected in cisterns around the house and farm.

They tried another farm in upstate New York, which eventually became the Maryfarm Retreat House. Finally, the Peter Maurin Farm was established on Staten Island. It was later moved to Tivoli and then eventually to Marlborough, both in the Hudson Valley.

Failing Farms

Peter, Dorothy, and their followers sincerely believed they could make the farms work. They couldn't. The reasons for the failure of the farming communes were many.

None of the earnest young people who joined had the slightest idea how to raise crops to feed large numbers. Peter and Dorothy's insistence on the rights of each individual to personal freedom resulted in frustrations: Someone who liked to drive a tractor, for example, might plow up all the crops that another had painstakingly planted.

Continual conflict between scholars and workers frayed the nerves. The workers wanted to "do," to work with their hands, while the scholars saw the farms as pleasant retreat centers. Neither could understand the other, and the friction between them was a great source of irritation for all.

Life on the farm was further complicated by the fact that "priests and sisters and other readers of the paper" sent "alcoholics or mental cases just out of a hospital," never thinking "to send money for their food." The farm staff was expected to raise the funds.[13] The people who were themselves attracted to the communal life were often those least suited to it—"the last people in the world capable of making a foundation, setting an example or leading a way," as Dorothy put it.[14]

There was the former drug addict who spoke several languages but refused to give language classes, instead spending his days inventing his own new language. The man who thought he was doing everyone a favor by stuffing damp driftwood, old shoes, and asbestos in the furnace. The boy dying of heart trouble whose family brought him to the farm for round-the-clock bed care.

[A] whole group ... used to go along the beach and collect clay from the banks. They enjoyed themselves (the idea was that they were practicing crafts) making dishes and bowls. This might have been viewed as a harmless and tranquilizing occupation, except that they were always washing the clay, their utensils, and their hands in the kitchen sink, frequently stopping up the plumbing.[15]

Ironically, in what was designed to be the ideal life for workers, the underlying problem with all the farmer communes seems to have been the presence of too many chiefs and not enough real workers. "None worked hard enough," Dorothy said. "No one worked as I have seen sisters and brothers in monasteries work."[16]

Food was particularly troublesome. Some of the commune members insisted on their own particular variety of bread or cereal. Others would eat nothing but red meat. At one time a fistfight broke out over a missing egg!

Still others wanted to be told what to do. Dorothy recalls one fellow who sat under a tree watching everyone else labor yet wouldn't lift a finger unless a "boss" came along. Since Peter and Dorothy were adamantly opposed to the idea of "bosses," he just sat there day in and day out.

Another man, when he heard a visiting priest say that attending Mass was the greatest work anyone could do, would go to Mass in the morning and then relax the rest of the day, expecting to be waited on because he had done the best work of all.

In the end—despite Dorothy's best attempts and the attempts of others who tried to emulate the experiment with varying degrees of success in other parts of the country—Peter's idea of "agronomic universities" spangling the American landscape faded into the obscurity that seems to be the fate of most communes.

Dorothy doesn't seem to have been torn up over the lack of success; indeed, she seems to have viewed the agricultural experiments as crosses between retreat centers and rural Houses of Hospitality. Probably the real reason for her lack of dismay was because her heart was never really rooted in the land; her love was with the urban worker. Now, though, one of her old passions was being resurrected by the specter of war, a passion that would send her to jail many more times and cost her the displeasure of many of her fellow Catholics.

TEN

War and Peace

Dorothy Day often said that if the bishop were to tell her to stop her work, she would immediately shut the doors, out of her loyalty to the Church and her respect for its authority. In light of that statement, these words from two of her critics are surprising:

No one can coerce you, except in matters of law and lawlessness, and this is not mine to judge. But as one who is proud of the title Catholic, I have the right to ask you to remove that proud name from your movement or place your movement in conformity with what the Church teaches.[1]

The Catholic Worker could have been a mecca for policies and programs to help the poor. Instead, it got off on the wrong track, and ended up in a cul de sac. Dorothy Day could have provided the experience for helping the poor, the racial minorities, and the alcoholics. Hundreds of groups and thousands of individuals could have been motivated by her to help the less fortunate. But instead of providing the practical knowledge and know-how that is needed the Catholic Worker went off on a tangent, where it could provide chaos, confusion, disruption, anarchy and a frightening disregard for authority.[2]

Confusion, disruption, and disregard for authority? Out of conformity with Church teaching? What would have prompted such accusations against Day?

In a word: pacifism.

Her position was simple, clear, and unwavering: "We are Christian pacifists and try to follow the counsels of perfection.... We firmly believe that our stand makes for the common good.... We may suffer for this faith, but we know that this suffering will be more fruitful than any words of ours."[3]

In fact, from her earliest days, even before her conversion, Dorothy adamantly opposed war in any form. Her first arrest had been her protest of the World War I draft, and she had been employed by the Anti-Conscription League before she became Catholic.

A Pacifist Paper

For the first three years of its life, *The Catholic Worker* quietly asserted its pacifism without much fanfare. It was a pacifist paper, but not out-spokenly so. Then, on its third anniversary, with the Spanish Civil War looming on the horizon, it made its (and Dorothy's) position apparent:

The Catholic Worker is sincerely a *pacifist* paper.... We oppose ... imperialist war. We oppose, moreover, preparedness for war, a preparedness which is going on now on an unprecedented scale and which will undoubtedly lead to war.... We must be brave enough and courageous enough to set the example.... A pacifist who is willing to endure the scorn of the unthinking mob, the ignominy of jail, the pain of stripes and the threat of death can not be lightly dismissed as a coward afraid of physical pain. A pacifist even now must be prepared for the opposition of the mob who thinks violence is bravery. The pacifist in the next war must be ready for martyrdom. We call upon youth to prepare.[4]

It was a radical position for a Catholic, since Catholics were being savagely attacked in Spain and a Catholic general, Francisco Franco, had led the resistance against the Loyalist central government.

The position of most American Catholics was clear: Franco was on the side of the Church—that is, the side of God—and therefore was in the right. The war was not only just, but necessary to save the lives of Catholics and to preserve the faith. There was no question where loyal Catholics should put their support, and there was no argument that the Spanish Civil War met St. Thomas Aquinas' criteria for a just war.

Dorothy vehemently disagreed:

Poor blood-drenched Spain is the most talked about subject today.... Who is right and who is wrong? We are inclined to believe that the issue is not so clear cut as to enable either side to condemn the other justifiably.... Our main concern is that the "members of Christ" tear one another;... Spain doesn't need favorable publicity for the rebels. She doesn't need condemnation of the loyalist. What she needs is the prayers of the rest of the Mystical Body. Please pray to God that Members will stop hating each other.... *The Catholic Worker* makes this appeal to its readers. Forget your anger. Let your indignation die. Remember only that the Body is rent asunder and the only solution is Love.[5]

The reaction to her editorial was swift and sharp. When *The Catholic Worker* was merely promoting good works, all was well, but this controversial stand was too much. Circulation fell by more than one hundred thousand, and *The Catholic Worker* was "excommunicated" by the Catholic Press Association. While a few supported her position of radical neutrality, many more American Catholics condemned it.

One typical letter to the editor read in part:

> I think that you are still a dirty Communist parading as a loyal Catholic.... I think, finally, that you are a two-faced hypocrite, a wolf in sheep's clothing, serving your Red monster, Joseph Stalin, who guides you from his capital at Moscow.... I hope to meet you in the dark some night, when you are accompanied by some of your "Red" butcher friends as I have a burning desire to achieve martyrdom for the Faith.[6]

An Unflinching Stand

Dorothy did not have a particularly thick skin, and such attacks cut deeply. Yet she was so convinced of the morality of her stand that she was undaunted, even when old friends from her socialist days condemned her. In 1938 she insisted, "As long as men trust to the use of force—only a superior, a more savage force, brutal force, will overcome the enemy." It was a position from which she never wavered.

In 1940, she wrote:

> Many of our readers ask, "What is the stand of *The Catholic Worker* in regard to the present war?" They are thinking as they

ask the question, of course, of the stand we took during the Spanish civil war. We repeat, that as in the Ethiopian war, the Spanish war, the Japanese and Chinese war, the Russian-Finnish war—so in the present war we stand unalterably opposed to war as a means of saving "Christianity," "civilization," "democracy." We do not believe that they can be saved by these means.[7]

Unquestionably she would have held the same position with regard to the Vietnam War, the Gulf War, and every other war America has been involved in.

Time and again, war after war, she urged Catholic workers to become conscientious objectors, and although she always insisted on the necessity of following one's own informed conscience, she was bitterly disappointed when some of her favorites opted to enlist. She was particularly grieved when her grandson Eric joined the Rangers and saw active duty in Vietnam.

Instead of participating in war, she urged, we should show greater loyalty to the Holy Father as soldiers of Christ in the spiritual battle that surrounds us daily.

What about our Holy Father as one of the heroes of the day? Do we wear buttons to remind us of our spiritual leader? Do we hang on his words with breathless interest and greet his every utterance with joy? Do we examine what he says, weigh his words, follow his leadership? Do we meditate on what he has said, do we ponder it prayerfully, do we try to serve under his banner as valiant soldiers of Christ? If we did there would be far more pacifists today, far more conscientious objectors.[8]

She went even further than merely to oppose combat. She asserted that it was morally reprehensible to make money off any kind of war effort.

There may be ever-improving standards of living in the United States, with every worker eventually owning his own home and driving his own car; but our whole modern economy is based on preparation for war, and this surely is one of the great arguments for poverty in our time. If the comfort one achieves results in the death of millions in the future, then that comfort shall be duly paid for. Indeed, to be literal, contributing to the war (misnamed "defense") effort is very difficult to avoid. If you work in a textile mill making cloth, or in a factory making dungarees or blankets, your work is still tied up with war. If you raise food or irrigate the land to raise food, you may be feeding troops or liberating others to serve as troops. If you ride a bus you are paying taxes. Whatever you buy is taxed, so that you are, in effect, helping to support the states' preparations for war exactly to the extent of your attachment to worldly things of whatever kind.[9]

Her total opposition to war persisted to the end of her life. She believed that in our modern times "of bombardment of civilians, open cities, the use of poison gas," the conditions for a "just war" could never be met. She even opposed the use of force to defend against invasion: "'And if we are invaded' is another question asked. We say again that we are opposed to all but the use of non-violent means to resist such an invader."[10]

Works of Mercy

Day urged "works of mercy rather than works of war," telling her readers:

> Instead of gearing ourselves in this country for a gigantic pro-
> duction of death-dealing bombers and men trained to kill, we
> should be producing food, medical supplies, ambulances, doctors
> and nurses for the works of mercy, to heal and rebuild a shattered
> world. Already there is famine in China. And we are still curtail-
> ing production in agriculture, thinking in terms of "price,"
> instead of human needs. We do not take care of our own unem-
> ployed and hungry millions in city and country, let alone those
> beyond the seas. There is prejudice in our own country towards
> Jews, Negroes, Mexicans, Filipinos and others, a sin crying to
> Heaven for punishment to care for the sick and the wounded, to
> the growing of food for the hungry, to the continuance of all our
> works of mercy in our houses and on our farms.[11]

She was not naively blind, however, to the inherent difficulties of her stance:

> We are urging what is a seeming impossibility—a training to the
> use of non-violent means of opposing injustice, servitude and a
> deprivation of the means of holding fast to the Faith. It is again
> the Folly of the Cross. But how else is the Word of God to be
> kept alive in the world. That Word is Love, and we are bidden
> to love God and to love one another. It is the whole law, it is all
> of life. Nothing else matters. Can we do this best in the midst of
> such horror as has been going on these past months by killing,
> or by offering our lives for our brothers?[12]

Not all her workers could follow her lead. Fifteen Houses of Hospitality closed in the months following the U.S. entry into World War II.

The Cold War Era

With the end of that war, America entered into the "Cold War," which Dorothy opposed just as vehemently as any "hot" war. She was particularly repelled by the annual civil defense drills held in anticipation of a nuclear attack. Her horror at the use of atomic weapons was palpable. She had written with uncharacteristic irony a month after Hiroshima and Nagasaki:

> Truman is a true man of his time in that he was jubilant. He was not a son of God, brother of Christ, brother of the Japanese, jubilating as he did.... We have killed 318,000 Japanese ... they are vaporizing, our Japanese brothers, scattered, men, women and babies, to the four winds, over the seven seas. Perhaps we will breathe their dust into our nostrils, feel them in the fog of New York on our faces, feel them in the rain on the hills of Easton.[13]

Given her opinion about nuclear weapons, it's not surprising that Dorothy would refuse to take part in state-sponsored drills. She not only believed it was futile to prepare for such an attack; she was convinced that having people practice for them gave the impression nuclear war was winnable and that the millions being spent on civil defense were morally defensible. So when the sirens blared in June 1955 to warn citizens to retreat to their designated shelters under the

New York State Defense Emergency Act, Dorothy and a handful of others sat in front of New York City Hall, refusing to budge.

"In the name of Jesus, who is God, who is Love," a Catholic Worker leaflet explained, "we will not obey this order to pretend, to evacuate, to hide. We will not be drilled into fear. We do not have faith in God if we depend upon the Atom Bomb."

The first year of their protest they were merely reprimanded. The next year they were jailed for five days. The next year the same judge sentenced them to thirty days. In 1958 they were again arrested, and a new judge suspended Dorothy's sentence. In 1959 she was jailed for five days.

In 1960 Dorothy and her little band had swelled to nearly five hundred. This time the police arrested only a few; Dorothy was not among them. In 1961, the final year of the civil defense drills, more than two thousand people protested; forty were arrested, but once again, Dorothy was singled out for exemption. In her own way, Dorothy had employed the techniques Martin Luther King Jr. would later advocate in the civil rights movement—and gained a small but significant victory.

With Liberty and Justice for All

Given her identification with the worker and her passion for justice, combined with her lifelong desire to see a new world order, it's not surprising that Dorothy was actively involved in the civil rights movement from the beginning. Her most dangerous moment came in 1957 when she visited Koinonia, an integrated Christian agricultural community in southwest Georgia. The Ku Klux Klan, angered by the close association of blacks and whites, had mounted an attack.

The community house had been fired on with machine guns, and crosses had been burned on the land. When Dorothy insisted on taking a turn as sentry, a speeding car fired a bullet at her. She ducked, and the bullet lodged in the steering wheel in front of her. She took the incident in stride, believing, as she always had, that in order to understand the plight of the downtrodden, one had to experience their life firsthand.

As the nation entered the turbulence of the sixties, more readers took umbrage with her positions on civil disobedience and her unrelenting pacifism. One day Roger La Porte, one of her admirers, doused himself with gasoline and set himself afire in opposition to the Vietnam War. Dorothy was horrified. Her pacifism most certainly extended to rejection of self-immolation, and the negative reactions La Porte's action caused the Catholic Worker grieved her deeply. She had not known him personally and was a bit affronted when people expected her to assume responsibility for his actions.

A Daughter of the Church

Concerned as always with war and peace, Day traveled to Rome during the Second Vatican Council as one of fifty "Mothers for Peace" who came to thank Pope John XXIII for his encyclical *Pacem in Terris*. Although they could not meet with him personally because he was so close to death, Dorothy and the others were blessed in a public audience. She returned to Rome yet another time in 1965 to take part in an unpublicized ten-day fast intended to encourage Council participants to make a strong statement on behalf of peace and against war.

Day saw the Council's *Constitution on the Church in the Modern*

World as an answer to that prayer. In this document, the bishops called any act of war "directed to the indiscriminate destruction of whole cities or vast areas with their inhabitants" as a "crime against God and humanity." It was the position she had held her entire adult life.

While encouraged by such small things, Dorothy was increasingly dismayed by the larger world. She had lived to see the beginning of a new order, but it was not the ordered and orderly world she had envisioned. This new world of changing sexual morality and free-floating protest had nothing to do with her vision of a society rooted in Christian principles and grounded in Christian ethics. She was so unhappy with the promiscuity and immorality in one Worker House apartment that in 1962 she tossed all the occupants out in what was later called the "The Dorothy Day Stomp." She found hippies "maddening" and was frustrated by their lack of wider vision.

She was no longer the cutting-edge young radical. She had become the matriarch of a movement, and the matriarch was feeling her age.

ELEVEN

GATHERING THE THREADS

Dorothy's final years were spent as she had spent most of her adult life—in caring for the poor, in writing, in dealing with financial concerns, in standing up for her principles. She took increasing comfort in her faith, especially attending Mass, writing, "the Mass begins our day, it is our food and drink, our delight, our refreshment, our courage, our light."[1] She spent more time on retreat, particularly enjoying those conducted under the direction of her spiritual advisor, Fr. John J. Hugo, who helped her view the Eucharist, prayer, and retreats as essential components in the great work of salvation in which all Christians are called to take part.

Although from time to time she imagined herself being alone in almost monastic solitude, her desire for community, her need to quell "the long loneliness," was stronger than her dreams of seclusion. She spent most of her old age either in one of the Catholic Worker communities or with her daughter, Tamar, and her family.

A Mother's Heart

What of Tamar, the child whose birth had allowed the Hound of Heaven finally to catch his prey?

A shy and retiring girl, Tamar was as much Forster's child as she was

Dorothy's. She preferred the quiet life in the country over the bustle of the city. Until her mother founded the Catholic Worker Movement, she had lived a relatively normal life. After that, she grew up in "community." It was an odd life, by any reckoning. Dorothy recalled:

> With the beginnings of the Catholic Worker, my working day began at early Mass ... and often ended at midnight. She [Tamar] was no longer my only one.... At night when visitors came, workers, scholars, priests, laymen, I left her in her bath and all but forgot her in the heat of discussion. In the delight of staying up late, Tamar stayed in the tub till the water was cold, making boats of the soap and her toys.[2]

Dorothy later mused, "Probably Tamar enjoyed the freedom my preoccupations gave her."

Tamar had no inclination for formal education. "She wanted to farm. She wanted to marry young and live on a farm,"[3] so despite Dorothy's reluctance, she arranged for Tamar to attend St. Martine's, an *Ecole Ménagère* outside Montreal where she could learn spinning, weaving, and how to make straw hats, in addition to some regular high school classes. Dorothy's displeasure about the situation is clear in *The Long Loneliness*: "Tamar wanted to try it, just to take the crafts, so one miserable fall day, we took the bus for Montreal and she was registered at the school."[4]

Dorothy was always torn between her love for her daughter and her responsibility for her, and her passion for serving the poor. After leaving Tamar at school, she wrote:

I never was so unhappy, never felt so great a sense of loneliness. She was growing up, she was growing up to be married. It did not seem possible. I was always having to be parted from her. No matter how many times I gave up mother, father, husband, brother, daughter for His sake, I had to do it over again.[5]

Tamar visited her mother on the weekends and during vacations. When she turned sixteen, Dorothy—undoubtedly remembering herself leaving for college at the same age—told Tamar she considered her to be "practically grown up."

Tamar stayed at St. Martine's for the winter, then moved to the Easton Community farm in the spring and summer. There she met Dave Hennessy, a roofer, who had come to the farm some months earlier. When it became apparent to Dorothy that their interest in each other had blossomed into romance, she moved Tamar back and forth between Mott Street and the farm, undoubtedly hoping that "out of sight, out of mind" would prevail. Unfortunately, absence made the heart grow fonder, and Tamar and Dave made plans to marry.

Dorothy was not pleased, but on the advice of Fr. Hugo, she gave her begrudging permission. She did insist that Tamar not marry before her eighteenth birthday, however. Tamar reluctantly agreed, but opted not to return to high school.

Instead, she spent time in a Catholic Worker household where she learned a great deal:

[How to] shop intelligently ... to buy and cook cheap cuts of meat, to bake and churn, keep a kitchen fire going, care for small animals in a back yard—rabbits, chickens, even white rats and canaries. She learned calligraphy and how to bind a book....

How to take care of the money you earned, how to earn money by caring for children, sitting with invalids, repainting murals in an old church.[6]

Despite her attempts to be positive about Tamar's life choice, Dorothy clearly had hoped for more from her only daughter. It was not to be. As soon as Tamar turned eighteen, she announced her engagement, and three weeks later, after the necessary banns had been announced at Sunday Mass, she and Dave were married at Easton farm.

It was a midweek wedding with few guests, and Tamar was afraid Peter Maurin would use the occasion for a lengthy indoctrination session on "pigs for profit." Despite Dorothy's best attempts to shush him, he did just that.

Later Dorothy would look back at his talk with a mixture of amusement and sorrow: "Our poor darling Peter! It was the last speech he made, as a matter of fact, because within a few months, he was stricken down, he lost his memory, and suddenly he could no longer 'think' as he tried to tell us."[7] His health would continue to decline, until five years later, suffering from severe dementia, he died at Easton farm.

Almost immediately Tamar and Dave began to have children— nine in all: Rebekah, Susannah, Eric, Nicholas, Mary, Margaret, Martha, Hilaire, and Catherine. It was not a happy relationship. They were chronically poor, often destitute. Hennessy was frequently unable to support his family because of his nervous temperament, and while Tamar did her best, she had few marketable skills.

Hennessy and Tamar separated a year after the birth of their last child. The breakup of the marriage and the lack of support from the Church led to Tamar's leaving the faith, something that grieved her mother unendingly. None of Dorothy's grandchildren or great-grand-children ever participated in the Catholic Worker Movement or even stayed connected to the Church.

Despite her sorrow over their choice, Dorothy remained close to her daughter and grandchildren, saying, "There is always an unspoken agreement, just as there was in my family of three brothers and a sister, parents and in-laws, not to dispute, not to argue, but to find points of agreement and concordances.... Not to judge, but to pray to understand."[8]

A Never-Ending Journey

In the waning years of her life, Dorothy continued to travel extensively, going as far as Australia, India, and Africa, and crisscrossing America. Despite a congestive heart, she kept up her work for the poor and dis-enfranchised. One of her last adventures was to be jailed when she joined Cesar Chavez's United Farm Workers demonstration against the Teamster's Union in August 1973.

Gradually, though, she withdrew from the affairs of the world. After 1976, she spent her time with Tamar and her grandchildren or at the Catholic Worker House on Third Street in New York, just a few blocks from the saloon where she and Eugene O'Neill and the other radicals of her youth had drunk the nights away and dreamed of a workers' revolution.

Dorothy lived long enough to see her work honored by the American Catholic Church. When she was seventy-five, *America* mag-azine dedicated an entire issue to her, praising her as the person who most exemplified "the aspiration and action of the American Catholic community during the past forty years." In 1972, Notre Dame University presented her with its highest honor, the prestigious Laetare Medal, in recognition of her "comforting the afflicted and afflicting the comfortable virtually all of her life."

Even before her death, she was being proclaimed a saint, something she rejected with disdain. "That's the way people try to dismiss you," she told an interviewer. "If you're a saint, then you must be impractical and utopian, and nobody has to pay any attention to you. That kind of talk makes me sick."[9]

The Hound of Heaven

Slowly, inexorably, her lifetime of sacrifice took its toll. She grew more frail and eventually became virtually bedridden. Tamar was with her when the Hound of Heaven crept near—"shade of His hand, outstretched caressingly," as Thompson had put it—at nightfall on November 29, 1980. There was no struggle, just the soft words, "Rise, clasp My hand, and come!"

Her funeral was held on December 2 at the Nativity Catholic Church, a half block from the Catholic Worker House where she died. The Church was filled with people who had loved and admired her, but behind her simple pine casket walked the three whom she had loved most of all on this earth: her daughter Tamar, her baby brother John, and Forster Batterham.

TWELVE

St. Dorothy?

In March 2000, Cardinal John J. O'Connor of New York announced that the Vatican had approved opening the cause for canonization for Dorothy Day. O'Connor said that her life, including her abortion, "speaks volumes" to women today since it shows that "a woman who had sinned so gravely" can become a woman of great "holiness and pacifism."

The question of whether Dorothy Day is a saint may take second seat to the question of whether she would want to be declared a saint. She often said, "Don't call me a saint. I don't want to be dismissed that easily!" Moreover, she undoubtedly would find the cost of the canonization process exorbitant, preferring that the money be spent on her beloved poor.

But such matters are now out of her hands, and the effort to declare her an official saint of the Church with a capital "S" is now underway. Meanwhile, her legions of admirers have little doubt that she is now one of the elect who see the face of God—a saint with a small "s." As one anonymous entry on the Catholic Worker website puts it: "If not Dorothy, then who?"

For those who support the formal declaration of sanctity, the Claretians offer the following prayer:

Prayer for the Canonization of Servant of God Dorothy Day

Merciful God, you called your servant Dorothy Day
    to show us the face of Jesus in the poor and forsaken.
By constant practice of the works of mercy,
    she embraced poverty
and witnessed steadfastly to justice and peace.
Count her among your saints
    and lead us all to become
friends of the poor ones of the earth,
    and to recognize you in them.
We ask this through your Son, Jesus Christ,
    bringer of good news to the poor. Amen.[1]

THIRTEEN

DOROTHY AND PETER

In the brief text "What the Catholic Worker Believes," Peter Maurin offered a straightforward statement of his vision for the movement.

The Catholic Worker believes
in the gentle personalism
of traditional Catholicism.
The Catholic Worker believes
in the personal obligation
of looking after
the needs of our brother.
The Catholic Worker believes
in the daily practice
of the Works of Mercy.
The Catholic Worker believes
in Houses of Hospitality
for the immediate relief
of those who are in need.
The Catholic Worker believes
in the establishment
of Farming Communes
where each one works
according to his ability

and gets
according to his need.
The Catholic Worker believes
in creating a new society
within the shell of the old
with the philosophy of the new,
which is not a new philosophy
but a very old philosophy
a philosophy so old
that it looks like new.[1]

Dorothy's own words, written about ten years after Peter's death, best describe him and his influence on her life.

When I first saw Peter Maurin my impression was of a short, broad-shouldered workingman with a high, broad head covered with graying hair. His face was weather beaten, he had warm grey eyes and a wide, pleasant mouth. The collar of his shirt was dirty, but he had tried to dress up by wearing a tie and a suit which looked as though he had slept in it. (As I found out afterward, indeed he had.)

What struck me first about him was that he was one of those people who talked you deaf, dumb and blind, who each time he saw you began his conversation just where he had left off at the previous meeting, and never stopped unless you begged for rest, and that was not for long. He was irrepressible and he was incapable of taking offense.

The night I met Peter I had come from an assignment for *The Commonweal*, covering the Communist-inspired "hunger march" of the unemployed to Washington. I had prayed at the Shrine of the

Immaculate Conception, on the Feast of the Immaculate Conception, that I might find something to do in the social order besides reporting conditions. I wanted to change them, not just report them, but I had lost faith in revolution, I wanted to love my enemy, whether capitalist or Communist.

I certainly did not realize at first that I had my answer in Peter Maurin. I was thirty-five years old and I had met plenty of radicals in my time and plenty of crackpots, too; people who had blueprints to change the social order were a dime a dozen around Union Square.

At that time Peter Maurin was fifty-seven, had never married, had been "away from the Church" in his youth, had worked with Sangnier and his social studies group in Paris, and had sold its paper, *Le Sillon*. He believed in going to the people in town and countryside, because first of all he was of the people himself.

He was born in a tiny hamlet in the southern part of France, two hundred miles from Barcelona, one of a family of twenty-four children. His own mother had died after she had borne her fifth child, and his stepmother had had nineteen and was still alive, he said.

"I did not like the idea of revolution," he once told me.

I did not like the French revolution, nor the English revolution. I did not wish to work to perpetuate the proletariat. I never became a member of a union, even though here in America I did all kinds of hard labor. I was always interested in the land and man's life on the land. That is why I went homesteading in Canada, but after two years, after my partner was killed in a hunting accident, I went around Canada with work gangs and entered this country in 1911, where I have been ever since.

When I first knew Peter, I was busy at a research job which kept me at the library until three in the afternoon. When I got home to my little apartment on East Fifteenth Street, I'd find him there waiting for me, ready to indoctrinate, to give me a lesson in history from the Catholic point of view. He had been sent to me, he said, by George Shuster, later president of Hunter College, who at that time was editor of *The Commonweal*. George thought that we were alike in point of view, both interested in changing the social order and in reaching the masses with the social teaching of the Church.

I had been a Catholic only about four years, and Peter, having suggested that I get out a paper to reach the man in the street, started right in on my education; he was a born teacher, and any park bench, coffee shop counter, bus or lodging house was a place to teach. He believed in starting on a program at once, without waiting to acquire classroom or office or meeting hall. To reach the man in the street, you went to the street. Peter was literal.

I had met Peter in December, 1932, and the first issue of *The Catholic Worker* came out in time for the May Day celebration in Union Square, 1933. What Peter Maurin was interested in was the publication of his essays, and my journalistic sense led me to report conditions as they were, to paint a picture of poverty and destitution, homelessness and unemployment, in short, to so arouse the conscience that the reader would be willing and ready to listen to Peter when he talked about things as they should be.

Peter was very much afraid of class war, and after his first essays were published he could not quite understand why I wrote so much about interracial injustice, hard conditions of labor, inadequate housing. He much preferred to write about how things should be—Houses of Hospitality for the needy, charity exercised in every home, voluntary poverty and the works of mercy, farming communes and agronomic universities that would teach people to earn a living by the sweat of their own brows instead of someone else's.

The Catholic Worker was financed like the publications of any radical "splinter group." If we had had a mimeograph machine, it would have been a mimeographed paper. But we had nothing but my typewriter, so we took our writing to a printer, found out it would cost $57 to get out 2,500 copies of a small, eight-page sheet the size of *The Nation,* and boldly had it set up. There were no office, no staff, no mailing list. I had a small paycheck coming in for the research job which was just finishing; two checks were due for articles I had written, but these were needed to pay overdue rent and light bills. Father Joseph McSorley, the Paulist, paid me generously for a small job of bibliography which I did for him; the late Father Ahearn, pastor of a black church in Newark, gave me ten dollars; Sister Peter Claver gave me one dollar which someone had just given her. Those were our finances. We took that first issue of the paper into Union Square that May Day and sold it for one penny a copy to Communists and trade unionists.

Peter slept in the back of *The Catholic Worker* office, and he soon brought in an Armenian anarchist poet and a German agnostic to share his quarters with him and to provide sparring partners for round-table discussions. He never took part in any of the work of the paper, except to turn in each month half a dozen "easy essays," many of which he insisted that we repeat over and over again. He was the kind of teacher who believed in repetition, restatement, and the continual return to first principles. He loved, however, to see visitors, and, if none came into the office, he went out into the highways and byways and found them.

The only time Peter got excited was when he found others agreeing with him, approving his ideas. Then his voice would rise, his eyes would shine and he would shout out exultingly. He always expected so much in the way of results that I often felt called upon to put a damper on him, to tone down his optimistic enthusiasms. But I soon noticed that he was never depressed or discouraged by disappointments or failures.

A failure such as that of the first round-table discussion was an example. Peter had hoped for great results from a series of Sunday afternoon discussions he had planned. Optimistically, for the first one he rented the ballroom of the Manhattan Lyceum, where trade union conventions as well as balls were often held. Only twenty people showed up; they gathered around the speaker's table and had an uproarious discussion on political action versus Catholic Action. After that, Peter rented a small meeting room. The waste of money, laboriously collected, did not bother him. There was plenty of money in the world, he believed. What was needed was men and women absorbed by the right ideas. Given the people, the money would follow. All one needed to do was to pray. When bills piled up and creditors came, we used to go to church and pray, all of us taking turns, and we called this "the picketing of St. Joseph." Once when I asked an unemployed chambermaid if she would take a half-hour of "picketing St. Joseph" over at Precious Blood Church, she asked me if she was to carry a sign. Once the printer sent us his bill with the notation, "Pray and pay!"

I asked Peter several times if he were not disappointed at the lack of success in indoctrinating the man on the street. I pointed to various examples of those who came to stay with us and whose condition seemed to get worse instead of better.

"People are just beginning to realize how deep-seated the evil is," he said soberly. "That is why we must be Catholic Radicals, we must get down to the roots. That is what radicalism is—the word means getting down to the roots."

Peter, even in his practicality, tried to deal with problems in the spirit of "the Prophets of Israel and the Fathers of the Church." He saw what the Industrial Revolution had done to human beings and he did not think that unions and organizations, strikes for higher wages and shorter hours, were going to be the solution. "Strikes don't strike me," he used to say when we went out to a picket line to distribute literature during a strike. But he came with us to hand out the literature—leaflets which dealt with men and women's dignity and their need and right to associate themselves with their fellows in trade unions, in credit unions, cooperatives, maternity guilds, etc.

He was interested in far more fundamental approaches. He liked the name "radical" and he had wanted the paper to be called *The Catholic Radical.* To him, *Worker* smacked of class war. What he wanted was to instill in all, worker or scholar, a philosophy of poverty and a philosophy of work.

He was the layman always. I mean that he never preached; he taught. While decrying secularism, the separation of the material from the spiritual, his emphasis as a layman was on our material needs, our need for work, food, clothing and shelter. Though Peter went weekly to confession and daily to Communion and spent an hour a day in the presence of the Blessed Sacrament, his study was of the material order around him. Though he lived in the city, he urged a return to the village economy, the study of the crafts and of agriculture. He was dealing with this world, in which God has placed us to work for a new heaven and a new earth wherein justice dwelleth.

He constantly urged individuals to practice the corporal and spiritual works of mercy; he urged bishops to establish Houses of

Hospitality. Somehow the two planks of the program got mixed up. I can remember well enough how it happened. He had written a series of essays addressed to the bishops, pointing out to them that canon law called for the establishment of hospices in every bishopric. When a reader who had been sleeping in the subway came into *The Catholic Worker* office one day and disclosed her need (the apartment and the office were already full), Peter's literal acceptance of "If thy brother needs food or drink, feed him, and if he needs shelter, shelter him" meant that we rented a large apartment a block away which became the first House of Hospitality for women. Now we have two houses, on First St. and Third St. Here the works of mercy are still being practiced by the group who get out *The Catholic Worker*, living without salaries, in voluntary poverty. "Feeding thy brother" started with feeding a few poor men. It became a daily breadline in 1936, and the line still forms every day outside the door.

Roundtable Discussions, Houses of Hospitality and Farming Communes—those were the three planks in Peter Maurin's platform. There are still Houses of Hospitality, each autonomous but inspired by Peter, each trying to follow Peter's principles. And there are farms, all different but all starting with the idea of the personalist and communitarian revolution—to use Emmanuel Mounier's phrase. Peter was not disappointed in his life's work. He had given everything he had and he asked for nothing, least of all for success. He gave himself, and—at the end—God took from him the power to think.

He was anointed at Easton for a bad heart condition, and a few years later, on May 15, 1949, he died at Maryfarm in Newburgh, New York. Garbed in a donated suit of clothes, he was buried in a donated grave in St. John's Cemetery, Brooklyn.

Obituaries were found not only in *The Industrial Worker*, a Chicago

I.W.W. paper which was on the subversive list, but also in *L'Osservatore Romano* in Vatican City, which carried its notice on the front page.

God has taken him into Paradise, with Lazarus who once was poor. May He bring us, too, to a place of refreshment, light and peace.[2]

FOURTEEN

In Her Words

A Selection of Quotes from the Published Writings of Dorothy Day

God gives us our temperaments, and in spite of my pacifism, it is natural for me to stand my ground to continue in what actually amounts to a class war, using such weapons as the works of mercy for immediate means to show our love and alleviate suffering.

The Long Loneliness

If we are rushed for time, sow time, and we will reap time. Go to church and spend a quiet hour in prayer. You will have more time than ever and your work will get done. Sow time with the poor. Sit and listen to them, give them your time lavishly. You will reap time a hundredfold. Sow kindness and you will reap kindness. Sow love, you will reap love.

The Long Loneliness

Ritual, how could we do without it! Though it may seem to be gibberish and irreverence, though the Mass is offered up in such haste that the sacred sentence, "*hoc est corpus meus,*" was abbreviated into "hocus-pocus" by the bitter protestor and has come down into our language meaning trickster, nevertheless there is a sureness and a conviction there. And just as a husband may embrace his wife casually as he leaves for work in the morning, and kiss her absent-mindedly in his comings and going, still that kiss on occasion turns to rapture, a burning fire of tenderness and love. And with this to stay her she demands the "ritual" of affection show. The little altar boy kissing the cruet of water as he hands it to the priest is performing a rite. We have too little ritual in our lives.

The Long Loneliness

St. Paul said that since the Fall nature itself travaileth and groaneth. So man has to contend with fallen nature in the beasts and in the earth as well as in himself. But when he overcomes the obstacles, he attains again to the joy of creativity.

The Long Loneliness

Because I sincerely loved His poor, He taught me to know Him. And when I think of the little I ever did, I am filled with hope and love for all those others devoted to the cause of social justice.

From Union Square to Rome[1]

Always the glimpses of God came most when I was alone. Objectors cannot say that it was fear of loneliness and solitude and pain that made me turn to Him. It was in those few years when I was alone and most happy that I found Him. I found Him at last through joy and thanksgiving, not through sorrow.

From Union Square to Rome

The experiences that I have had are more or less universal. Suffering, sadness, repentance, love, we all have known these. They are easiest to bear when one remembers their universality, when we remember that we are all members or potential members of the Mystical Body of Christ.

From Union Square to Rome

A conversion is a lonely experience. We do not know what is going on in the depths of the heart and soul of another. We scarcely know ourselves.

From Union Square to Rome

Someone once described me in an interview as "authoritative." Later, listening to a tape recording of a talk I had given on the plight of agricultural workers, I had to admit that I did sound didactic. Since then, I have tried to be more gentle in my approach to others, so as not to make them feel that I am resentful of their comfort when I speak of the misery of the needy and the groaning of the poor.

Loaves and Fishes (86)[2]

Poverty is a strange and elusive thing. I have tried to write about it, its joys and sorrows, for thirty years now; and I could probably write about it for another thirty without conveying what I feel about it as well as I would like. I condemn poverty and I advocate it; poverty is simple and complex at once; it is a social phenomenon and a personal matter. Poverty is an elusive thing, and a paradoxical one.

Loaves and Fishes (71)

Easiest of all is to have so little, to have given away so much, that there is nothing left to give. But is this ever true? This point of view leads to endless discussions; but the principle remains the same. We *are* our brother's keeper. Whatever we have beyond our own needs belongs to the poor. If we sow sparingly we will reap sparingly. And it is sad but true that we must give far more than bread, than shelter.

Loaves and Fishes (92)

Most of us are inclined to shrug and say with St. Teresa of Avila, "All times are dangerous times," and to settle down to our daily affairs, trusting God to take care of everything. So long as we say a few prayers each day, get to Mass, and go on living our comfortable lives, we feel secure because we have "faith."

Loaves and Fishes (122)

And of course we have made mistakes. We have erred often in judgment and in our manner of writing and presenting the truth as we see it. I mean the truth about the temporal order in which we live and in which, as laymen, we must play our parts. I am not speaking of "truths of the faith," which we accept not only because they are reasonable to believe but because the Holy Mother Church has presented them to us. The Church is infallible when it deals with truths of the faith such as the dogma of the Immaculate Conception and the Assumption of the Blessed Virgin Mary. When it comes to concerns of the temporal order—capital vs. labor, for example—on all these matters the Church has not spoken infallibly. Here is room for wide differences of opinion.

Loaves and Fishes (122)

There are many times when I grow impatient at the luxury of the Church, the building programs, the cost of the diocesan school system, and the conservatism of the hierarchy. But then I think of our priests. What would we do without them? They are so vital a part of our lives, standing by us as they do at birth, marriage, sickness, and death—at all the great and critical moments of our existence—but also daily bringing us the bread of life, our Lord Himself, to nourish us. "To whom else shall we go?" we say with St. Peter.

Loaves and Fishes (126)

When I lay in jail thinking of these things, thinking of war and peace and the problem of human freedom, of jails, drug addiction, prostitution, and the apathy of great masses of people who believe that nothing can be done—when I thought of these things I was all the more confirmed in my faith in the little way of St. Thérèse. We do the things that come to hand, we pray our prayers and beg also for an increase of faith—and God will do the rest.

Loaves and Fishes (178)

Thank God for retroactive prayer! St. Paul said that he did not judge himself, nor must we judge ourselves. We can turn to our Lord Jesus Christ, who has already repaired the greatest evil that ever happened or could ever happen, and trust that He will make up for our falls, for neglects, for our failures in love.

Loaves and Fishes (184)

It takes some time to calm one's heart, which fills all too easily with irritation, resentment, and anger. But there, in the quiet of the chapel, looking around at the work done by those same men who caused the irritation, it is easier to adjust one's thoughts.

Loaves and Fishes (208)

The greatest challenge of the day is: how to bring about a revolution of the heart, a revolution which has to start with each one of us? When we begin to take the lowest place, to wash the feet of others, to love our brothers with that burning love, that passion, which led to the Cross, then we can truly say, "Now I have begun." Day after day we accept our failure, but we accept it because of our knowledge of the victory of the Cross. God has given us our vocation, as He gave it to the small boy who contributed his few loaves and fishes to help feed the multitude, and which Jesus multipled so that He fed five thousand people.

Loaves and Fishes (215)

I should know by this time that just because I *feel* that everything is useless and going to pieces and badly done and futile, it is not really that way at all. Everything is all right. It is in the hands of God. Let us abandon everything to Divine Providence.

House of Hospitality [3]

Oh dear, I am reminded of St. Teresa who said, "The devil sends me so offensive a bad spirit of temper that at times I think I could eat people up." I'm glad that she felt that way, too. St. Thomas said there is no sin in having a righteous wrath provided there is no undue desire for revenge.

House of Hospitality

When we are comfortable, beware. It is only when things are hard that we are making progress. God is good to send trials. They are a special mark of love.... Those circumstances which surround us are the very ones God wills for us.

House of Hospitality

Poverty means lack of paint, it means bedbugs, cockroaches and rats and the constant war against these. Poverty means body lice. A man fainted on the coffee line some months ago and just holding his head to pour some coffee between his drawn lips meant picking up a few bugs. Poverty means lack of soap and Lysol and cleansing powders.

The Catholic Worker[4]

Our work is to sow. Another generation will be reaping the harvest.

"Aims and Purposes"[5]

It is a good thing to ask honestly what you would do, or have done, when a beggar asked at your house for food. Would you—or did you—give it on an old cracked plate, thinking that was good enough? Do you think that Martha and Mary thought that the old and chipped dish was good enough for their guest?

"Room for Christ"[6]

One tragedy of today [is] a loss of the joy of life, joy in living, which men should have if they were healthy and happy.

The Third Hour, 1949

But we repeat, we proclaim, that we do see results from our personal experiences and we proclaim our faith. Christ has died for us. Adam and Eve fell, and Juliana [of Norwich] wrote, the worst has already happened and been repaired. Christ continues to die in His martyrs all over the world, in His Mystical Body, and it is this dying, not the killing in wars, which will save the world.

The Catholic Worker[7]

You can strip yourself, and you can be stripped ... but still you are going to reach out like an octopus and seek your own. Your comfort, your ease, your refreshment, and it may mean books and music, the interior senses being gratified, or it may mean food and drink. One giving up is no easier than the other. Cups of coffee, cigarettes, jealousy of time, etc.

"Poverty Is to Care and Not to Care"[8]

Yes, the poor we are always going to have with us, Our Lord told us that, and there will always be a need for our sharing, for stripping ourselves to help others. It will always be a lifetime job. But I am sure that God did not intend there be so many poor. The class structure is of our making and our consent, not His. It is the way we have arranged it, and so it is up to us to change it. So we are urging revolutionary change.

"Poverty Is to Care and Not to Care"[9]

There have been many sins against the poor which cry out to high heaven for vengeance. The one listed as one of the seven deadly sins is depriving the laborer of his share. There is another one, that is, instilling in him the paltry desires to satisfy that for which he must sell his liberty and his honor. Not that we are not all guilty of concupiscence, but newspapers, radios, television, and battalions of advertising people (woe to that generation) deliberately stimulate his desires, the satisfaction of which means the degradation of the family.

"Poverty Is to Care and Not to Care"[10]

We who live in this country cannot be as poor as those who go out to other countries. This is so rich a country that luxury has developed at the expense of necessities, and even the destitute partake of the luxury. We are the rich country of the world, like Dives at the feast. We must try hard, we must study to be poor like Lazarus at the gate, who was taken into Abraham's bosom. The Gospel doesn't tell us anything about Lazarus' virtues. He just sat there and let the dogs lick his sores. He would be classed by any social worker of today as a mental case. But again, poverty and in this case destitution, like hospitality, is so esteemed by God, it is something to be sought after, worked for, the pearl of great price.

"Poverty Is the Pearl of Great Price"[11]

What about this business of letting the other fellow get away with it? Isn't there something awfully smug about such piety—building up your own sanctification at the expense of an increased guilt of someone else? This turning the other cheek, this inviting someone else to be a potential murderer, or thief, in order that we may grow in grace— how obnoxious! In that case I'd rather be the striker than the meek one struck. One would all but rather be a sinner than a saint at the expense of the sinner. In other words, we must be saved together.

The Catholic Worker [12]

I always say to the Blessed Mother after Communion—"Here He is in my heart; I believe, help thou mine unbelief; Adore Him, thank Him and love Him for me. He is your Son; His honor is in your hands. Do not let me dishonor Him."

The Catholic Worker [13]

It is no easier to receive a hearing with princes of the Church than it is to receive one from the princes of this world. There is protocol; there is hierarchy and blocs of one kind or another, there is diplomacy in what we generally consider to be the realm of the spirit.

The Catholic Worker [14]

I am a traditionalist, in that I do not like to see Mass offered with a large coffee cup as a chalice.

The Catholic Worker[15]

God is on the side even of the unworthy poor.

The Catholic Worker[16]

There is ... [tremendous freedom] in the Church, a freedom most cradle Catholics do not seem to know they possess. They do know that a man is free to be a Democrat or a Republican, but they do not know that he is also free to be a philosophical anarchist by conviction. They do believe in free enterprise, but they do not know that cooperative ownership and communal ownership can live side by side with private ownership of property.

Ave Maria

Obedience is a matter of love, which makes it voluntary, not compelled by fear or force. Pope John's motto was "Obedience and Peace." Yet he was the pope who flouted conventions which had hardened into laws as to what a pope could or could not do and the Pharisees were scandalized and the people delighted.

Ave Maria

How can we believe in a Transcendent God when the Immanent God seems so powerless within time, when demonic forces seem to be let loose? Certainly our God is a hidden God.

"What Do the Simple Folk Do?"[17]

All men are brothers, yes, but how to love your brother or sister when they are sunk in ugliness, foulness, and degradation, so that all the senses are affronted? How to love when the adversary shows a face to you of implacable hatred, or just cold loathing?

"What Do the Simple Folk Do?"[18]

We must remember that faith, like love, is an act of the will, an act of preference. God speaks, He answers these cries in the darkness as He always did. He is incarnate today in the poor, in the bread we break together. We know Him and each other in the breaking of bread.

"What Do the Simple Folk Do?"[19]

Catholics do not generally ask for miracles. They leave the extraordinary in the hands of God. They are quite conscious that before prayer of petition there must be offered prayer of adoration and thanksgiving as their bounden duty to a Creator and to themselves. Spiritual graces, yes, they ask for these, but when it comes to asking for relief from pain and suffering, it is almost as though they thought, "Why should I refuse what is the common lot of humanity? Why should I ask to be spared when I see the suffering of the family next door?" Suffering borne with courage means to the devout mind a participation in the suffering of Christ and, if bravely endured, can lighten the suffering of others. It is not a cult of suffering. It is an acceptance of the human condition.

"What Do the Simple Folk Do?"[20]

In a way of course taking care of your own, children and grandchildren, is taking care of your self. On the other hand, there is the sacrament of duty, as Father McSorley calls it. There is great joy in being on the job, doing good works, performing the works of mercy. But when you get right down to it, a work which is started personally often ends up by being paper work—writing letters, seeing visitors, speaking about the work while others do it. One can become a veritable Mrs. Jellyby [a character in *Bleak House,* by Charles Dickens], looking after the world and neglecting one's own who are struggling with poverty and hard work and leading, as such families with small children do these days, ascetic lives. There are vigils, involuntary ones, fasting due to nausea of pregnancy, for instance, but St. Angela of Foligno said that penances voluntarily undertaken are not half so meritorious as those imposed on us by the circumstances of our lives and cheerfully borne.

On Pilgrimage[21]

Every time I am making what I consider a thorough confession—that is, telling tendencies that I wish I could overcome, like eating between meals, indulging in the nibbling that women do around a kitchen, and I mention it in confession as a venial sin not only in regard to myself but my neighbor who is starving all over the world, the confessor makes no attempt to understand, but speaks of scruples. One confessor said, "I order you to eat between meals!"

On Pilgrimage

Moreover, much as I love St. Peter's mother-in-law and how "she rose and ministered to them," and much as I love St. Paul's talk of grandmothers, I know that mother-in-law and grandmother should not be too much in evidence or trying to live the lives of the younger people. If we are there to serve, it is one thing. But usually we are not nearly so much needed as we think we are. There are such things as guardian angels, and our dear Lord watches over all.

On Pilgrimage

If these jobs do not contribute to the common good, we pray God for the grace to give them up. Have they to do with shelter, food, clothing? Have they to do with the works of mercy? Everyone should be able to place his job in the category of the works of mercy.

This would exclude jobs in advertising, which only increase people's useless desires. In insurance companies and banks, which are known to exploit the poor of this country and of others. Banks and insurance companies have taken over land and built huge collective farms, ranches, plantations, of 30,000, 100,000 acres, and have dispossessed the poor man. Loan and finance companies have further defrauded him. Movies [and] radio have further enslaved him. So that he has no time nor thought to give to his life, either of soul or body. Whatever has contributed to the misery and degradation of the poor may be considered a bad job, and not to be worked at. If we examine our conscience in this way, we would soon be driven into manual labor, into humble work, and so would become more like our Lord and our Blessed Mother.

On Pilgrimage

Poverty means non-participation. It means what Peter calls regional living. This means fasting from tea, coffee, cocoa, grapefruit, pineapple etc. from things not grown in the region where one lives.

"Poverty and Pacifism"[22]

One more sin, O suffering Christ, worker Yourself, for You to bear. In the garden of Gethsemane, You bore the sins of all the world—You took them on Yourself, the sins of those police, the sins of the Girdlers, and the Schwabs, of the Graces of this world. In committing them, whether ignorantly or of their own free will, they piled them on Your shoulders, bowed to the ground with the weight of the guilt of the world, which You assumed because You loved each of us so much. You took them on Yourself, and You died to save us all. Your precious Blood was shed even for that policeman whose cudgel smashed again and again the skull of that poor striker, whose brains lay splattered on the undertaker's slab.

"Who Is Guilty of Murders in Chicago?" [23]

If we do not keep indoctrinating, we lose the vision. And if we lose the vision, we become merely philanthropists, doling out palliatives.

"Aims and Purposes" [24]

We are not going to win the masses to Christianity until we live it.

The Catholic Worker [25]

Weaving is her [Tamar's] "tranquilizer." Knitting generally is mine, though I never get beyond scarves. I have made socks for the children, and once in a while achieved a good pair for an adult. One monstrosity I made which would match nothing and was due to be ripped out was seized by Ann Marie as an amusing gift (together with one of her own perfect ones) for a Worker Priest. I hope by now some friendly soul has re-knit it for him.

The Catholic Worker [26]

These are great mysteries. Most of the time we do not comprehend at all. Sometimes the Holy Spirit blows upon us and chases some of the fog away and we see a bit more clearly. But most of the time we see through a glass darkly. Our need to worship, to praise, to give thanksgiving, makes us return to the Mass daily, as the only fitting worship which we can offer to God. Having received our God in the conse-crated bread and wine, which still to sense is bread and wine, it is now not we ourselves who do these things except by virtue of the fact that we will to do them, and put ourselves in the position to do them by coming to the Holy Sacrifice, receiving communion, and then with Christ in our hearts and literally within us in the bread we have received, giving this praise, honor and glory and thanksgiving.

"The Council and the Mass"[27]

One must follow one's own conscience first before all authority, and of course, one must inform one's conscience. But one must follow one's conscience still, even if it is an ill-informed one.

The Catholic Worker [28]

Yes, reading is prayer—it is searching for light on the terrible problems of the day, at home and abroad, personal problems and national prob-lems, that bring us suffering of soul and mind and body.

And relief always comes. A way is opened, "Seek and you shall find."

The Catholic Worker [29]

And finally, this summation of her life and her work:

The mystery of the poor is this: That they are Jesus, and what you do for them you do for Him. It is the only way we have of knowing and believing in our love. The mystery of poverty is that by sharing in it, making ourselves poor in giving to others, we increase our knowledge of and belief in love.

"The Mystery of the Poor" [30]

NOTES

One
In the Beginning

1. Dorothy Day, *The Long Loneliness* (New York: Harper & Row San Francisco, 1952), 31. Hereafter cited as *Loneliness.*

2. Dorothy Day, *House of Hospitality* [n.p.], available online at Dorothy Day Library on the Web, www.catholicworker.org. This text, like many of Day's writings, is not copyrighted and appears online without page numbers.

3. Robert Ellsberg, ed., *By Little and by Little: The Selected Writings of Dorothy Day* (Maryknoll, N.Y.: Orbis, 1992), 183.

4. *Loneliness,* 11.

5. *Loneliness,* 28.

6. *Loneliness,* 19.

7. *Loneliness,* 20.

8. She is called Mary Harrington in *The Long Loneliness.*

9. *Loneliness,* 24.

10. *Loneliness,* 28.

11. Dorothy Day, "On Pilgrimage—June 1972," *The Catholic Worker* [hereafter cited as *CW*], June 1972, 2, 7. The texts of *The Catholic Worker* are in the public domain and appear online, with pages unnumbered, at the Dorothy Day Library on the Web, www.catholicworker.org.

12. Dorothy Day, "On Pilgrimage—June 1972," *CW,* June 1972, 34.

13. Dorothy Day, *From Union Square to Rome*, [n. p.], available online at the Dorothy Day Library on the Web, www.catholic worker.org/dorothyday/. Hereafter cited as *Union Square*.

Two
Growing Up Radical

1. *Loneliness*, 43.
2. *Loneliness*, 43.
3. *Loneliness*, 46.
4. *Loneliness*, 49.
5. *Loneliness*, 62.
6. *Loneliness*, 60.
7. *Loneliness*, 55-56.
8. *Loneliness*, 66.
9. *Loneliness*, 58.

Three
The Greatest Sorrow of All

1. *Loneliness*, 78.
2. *Loneliness*, 83.
3. *Loneliness*, 84.
4. *Loneliness*, 93.
5. Dorothy Day, "On Pilgrimage—September 1963," *CW,* September 1986, 1, 2, 6, 8.
6. Dorothy Day, "An Open Letter to Fr. Dan Berrigan," *CW,* December 1972.

Four
Love Is the Measure of All

1. *Loneliness,* 94-95.
2. *Loneliness,* 95.
3. *Loneliness,* 95.
4. *Loneliness,* 100.
5. Occoquan was the prison where she had been held after the suffragist march.
6. *Loneliness,* 104.
7. *Loneliness,* 105.
8. *Loneliness,* 106.
9. *Loneliness,* 113.
10. Dorothy Day, "To Die for Love," *CW,* September 1948, 2, 8.
11. *Loneliness,* 134.
12. *Loneliness,* 120.
13. *Loneliness,* 148.
14. *Loneliness,* 148.
15. *Loneliness,* 133.

Five
A Child Is Born

1. *Union Square* [n. p.].
2. Dorothy Day, "The Family vs. Capitalism," *CW,* January 1936, 4.
3. *Loneliness,* 136.
4. Dorothy Day, "On Pilgrimage—October/November 1975," *CW,* October–November 1975, 1, 8.

5. *Loneliness,* 148.
6. *Loneliness,* 147.
7. Ellsberg, 64.
8. The deaths of Sacco and Vanzetti were a watershed in American xenophobia of the 1920s. On April 15, 1920, a factory paymaster in South Braintree, Massachusetts, was robbed of $15,776. Three weeks later, on May 5, 1920, two Italians, Nicola Sacco and Bartolomeo Vanzetti, were accused of the crime. In what became the century's most notorious criminal trial, the two were sentenced to death, not because of their involvement in the robbery (which continues to be debated to this day), but because of their anarchist activities. Worldwide protests of the unfairness of their trial were to no avail. They were executed on August 23, 1927.
9. *Loneliness,* 147.
10. *Loneliness,* 147.
11. *Loneliness,* 140.

Six

The Cost of Conversion

1. *Union Square* [n. p.].
2. *Loneliness,* 149.
3. *Loneliness,* 149.
4. *Loneliness,* 150.
5. *Loneliness,* 150.
6. Robert Coles, M.D., *Dorothy Day: A Radical Devotion* (Reading, Mass.: Addison-Wesley, 1987), 58.
7. *Loneliness,* 150.
8. *CW,* June 1967.

9. *Loneliness,* 236.

10. Dorothy Day, *On Pilgrimage* (Grand Rapids, Mich.: Eerdmans, 1999), 100.

11. Dorothy Day, "Poverty Is the Pearl of Great Price," *CW,* July–August 1953, 1, 7.

12. *Union Square* [n. p.].

13. *Loneliness,* 165.

14. *Loneliness,* 166.

Seven
An Unlikely Mentor

1. William D. Miller, *Dorothy Day: A Biography* (San Francisco: Harper & Row, 1982), 247.

2. *Loneliness,* 178.

3. *Loneliness,* 179.

4. Dorothy Day, *Loaves and Fishes* (Maryknoll, N.Y.: Orbis, 1963), 85. Hereafter cited as *Loaves.*

5. *Loaves,* 105.

6. *Loaves,* 5.

7. *Loaves,* 5-6.

8. Peter Maurin, *Easy Essays,* available online at the Dorothy Day Library on the Web, www.catholicworker.org.

9. *Loaves,* 7.

10. *Loaves,* 7.

11. *Loaves,* 7.

12. *Loaves,* 13.

Eight
Work for the Worker

1. Dorothy Day, "Poverty and Precarity," *CW,* May 1952, 2, 6.
2. Dorothy Day, "To Our Readers," *CW,* May 1933, 4 (first issue).
3. Day, "To Our Readers," 4.
4. *Loaves,* 19.
5. *Loneliness,* 172.
6. *Loaves,* 20.
7. Dorothy Day, "Maurin's Program," *CW,* June–July 1933, 4.
8. *Loaves,* 23.
9. *Loneliness,* 182.
10. Dorothy Day, "On Pilgrimage—June 1975," *CW,* (June 1975), 1, 2, 6.
11. Day, *House of Hospitality* [n. p.].
12. Dorothy Day, "Day After Day," *CW,* November 1933, 1, 2.
13. *Loaves,* 26.
14. Dorothy Day, "Room for Christ," *CW,* December 1945, 2.

Nine
Together We Stand

1. *Loaves,* 29.
2. *Loaves,* 30.
3. *Loaves,* 31.
4. Dorothy Day, "Day After Day—May 1934," CW (May 1934), 1, 2.
5. Quoted in Miller, 289.

6. *Loaves,* 35-37.

7. *Loaves,* 37.

8. *Loaves,* 39.

9. Dorothy Day, "Day After Day—September 1942," *CW,* September 1942, 1, 2.

10. *Loaves,* 43.

11. *Loaves,* 44.

12. *Loaves,* 44.

13. *Loaves,* 51.

14. *Loaves,* 48.

15. *Loaves,* 59.

16. Miller, 294.

Ten

War and Peace

1. Frank Morris, "Strings to the Bow: An Open Letter to Dorothy Day," *Register,* November 19, 1965, [n. p.].

2. Daniel Lyons, S.J."Right or Wrong: Dorothy Day and the Catholic Worker," *Our Sunday Visitor* [n. d.].

3. Dorothy Day, "Pacifism," *CW,* May 1936, 8.

4. Dorothy Day, "The Mystical Body and Spain," *CW,* August 1936, 4.

5. "Letters to the Editor," *CW,* September 1936 [n. p.].

6. Dorothy Day, "Explains CW Stand on Use of Force," *CW,* September 1938, 1, 4, 7.

7. Dorothy Day, "Our Stand," *CW,* June 1940, 1, 4.

8. Dorothy Day, "Day After Day—April 1942," *CW,* April 1942, 1, 4.

9. *Loaves,* 86.

10. Day, "Our Stand," 1, 4.

11. Day, "Our Stand," 1, 4.

12. Day, "Our Stand," 1, 4.

13. Dorothy Day, "We Go on Record: The CW Response to Hiroshima," *CW,* September 1945, 1.

Eleven
Gathering the Threads

1. Dorothy Day, "The Council and the Mass," *CW,* September 1962, 2.

2. *Loneliness,* 237.

3. *Loneliness,* 239.

4. *Loneliness,* 239.

5. *Loneliness,* 239.

6. *Loneliness,* 240.

7. *Loneliness,* 242.

8. Miller, 492.

9. Jim Gallagher, "Dorothy Day: A Worker's Labor of Love for the Poor," *Chicago Tribune* (March 23, 1977).

Twelve
St. Dorothy?

1. Distributed by Claretian Publications, 205 W. Monroe St., Chicago, IL 60606, editors@uscatholic.org. 312-236-7782 ext. 474;

Thirteen
Dorothy and Peter

1. This text originally appeared numerous times in *CW* and is reprinted in Nancy L. Roberts, *Dorothy Day and the Catholic Worker* (Albany, N.Y.: State University of New York, 1984).
2. With minor revisions from the preface to the 1961 edition of Dorothy Day, *The Green Revolution*, available from the Dorothy Day Library on the Web at www.catholicworker.org/dorothyday/. In the public domain.

Fourteen
In Her Words

1. Quotes in this chapter from the book *From Union Square to Rome* are from chapter one, pp. 1-17, available online at www.catholic-worker.org/dorothyday/.
2. The number in parentheses after a book title gives the page where the quote is found in the original text.
3. Quotes from *House of Hospitality* come from the text that appears online at the Dorothy Day Library at: www.catholicworker.org/dorothyday/.
4. Dorothy Day, "Funds Needed to Carry on Work in N.Y.," *CW*, September 1939, 1, 4. Quotes from *The Catholic Worker* can be accessed online at the Dorothy Day Library on the Web, www.catholicworker.org/dorothyday/.
5. *CW*, February 1940, 7.
6. *CW*, December 1945, 2.
7. "Inventory—January 1951," *CW*, January 1951, 1, 2.

8. *CW,* April 1953, 1, 5. Day always carried a jar of instant coffee with her and smoked until her mid-forties.

9. *CW,* April 1953, 1, 5.

10. *CW,* April 1953, 1, 5.

11. *CW,* August 1953, 1, 7.

12. "A Friend of the Family—Mr. O'Connell Is Dead," *CW,* March 1952, 1, 6.

13. *CW,* November 5, 1943.

14. "On Pilgrimage—June 1963," *CW,* June 1963, 1, 2, 6, 8.

15. "On Pilgrimage—March 1966," *CW,* March 1966, 1, 2, 6, 8.

16. "On Pilgrimage—February 1968," *CW,* February 1968, 2, 8.

17. *CW,* May 1978, 5, 8.

18. *CW,* May 1978, 5, 8.

19. *CW,* May 1978, 5, 8.

20. *CW,* May 1978, 5, 8.

21. Quotes from *On Pilgrimage* come from the text that appears online at the Dorothy Day Library at www.catholicworker.org/dorothyday/.

22. *CW,* December 1944, 1, 7.

23. *CW,* July 1937, 1, 4, 7.

24. *CW,* February 1940, 7.

25. "On Pilgrimage—December 1961," *CW,* December 1961, 1, 2, 7.

26. "On Pilgrimage—January 1962," *CW,* January 1962, 1, 7, 8.

27. *CW,* September 1962, 2.

28. "On Pilgrimage—Our Spring Appeal," *CW,* May 1970, 1, 2, 11.

29. "On Pilgrimage—July/August 1973," *CW,* July–August 1973, 2, 7.

30. *CW,* April 1964, 2.

SELECTED BIBLIOGRAPHY

The Catholic Worker. 1933 to the present.

Coles, Robert. *Dorothy Day: A Radical Devotion.* Reading, Mass.: Addison-Wesley, 1987.

Day, Dorothy. *Loaves and Fishes.* Maryknoll, N.Y.: Orbis, 1963.

————. *The Long Loneliness.* San Francisco: Harper San Francisco, 1952.

————. *On Pilgrimage.* Grand Rapids, Mich.: Eerdmans, 1999.

Ellsberg, Robert. *By Little and by Little: The Selected Writings of Dorothy Day.* Maryknoll, N.Y.: Orbis, 1999.

Forest, Jim. "A Biography of Dorothy Day." Online at www.catholicworker.org.

Gallagher, Jim. "Dorothy Day: A Worker's Labor of Love for the Poor." *Chicago Tribune* (March 23, 1977).

Garvey, Michael. *Dorothy Day: Selections From Her Writings.* Springfield, Ill.: Templegate, 1966.

Lyons, Daniel. "Right or Wrong: Dorothy Day and the Catholic Worker," Huntington, Ind.: *Our Sunday Visitor,* no date.

Merriman, Brigid O'Shea. *Searching for Christ: The Spirituality of Dorothy Day.* Notre Dame, Ind.: University of Notre Dame Press, 1994.

Miller, William D. *Dorothy Day: A Biography.* San Francisco: Harper & Row, 1982.

Morris, Charles. *American Catholic.* New York: Vintage, 1997.

Morris, Frank. "Strings to the Bow: An Open Letter to Dorothy Day." *Register* (Nov 19, 1965).

O'Connor, June E. *The Moral Vision of Dorothy Day: A Feminist Perspective.* New York: Crossroad, 1991.

Roberts, Nancy L. *Dorothy Day and the Catholic Worker.* Albany, N.Y.: State University of New York, 1984.

Vishnewski, Stanley. *Meditations: Dorothy Day.* New York: Newman, 1970.

Westenhaver, Edythe. "Dorothy Day Views the Council." *St. Louis Review* (October 8, 1965).

Zagano, Phyllis. *Woman to Woman: An Anthology of Women's Spiritualities.* Collegeville, Minn.: Liturgical, 1993.

Meet the Saints Series

Cynthia Cavnar, *Meet Edith Stein*

George Kosicki, *Meet Saint Faustina*

Mary van Balen Holt, *Meet Katharine Drexel*

Patricia Treece, *Meet Padre Pio*

Brother Leo Wollenweber, *Meet Solanus Casey*